HELP ME
STOP OVERTHINKING

THE ULTIMATE GUIDE TO STOP OVERTHINKING

AND LIVE YOUR BEST LIFE

VAUGHN CARTER

FURTHER TOGETHER PUBLISHING

CONTENTS

INTRODUCTION

Have you ever found yourself lying in bed, staring at the ceiling, unable to silence the relentless chatter of your mind? Or perhaps you've spent countless hours analyzing past conversations, worrying about the future, and second-guessing every decision you've ever made? Remember, many of us are in the same boat. In fact, you're in the company of millions who have fallen victim to a relentless and often paralyzing mental habit: overthinking.

Welcome to *Help Me Stop Overthinking*—a book designed to be your trusted companion on the journey to reclaiming your peace of mind. I'm thrilled to be your guide, and if you've read my previous works, *Help Me I'm Stuck* and *Help Me Talk to Anyone*, you know that I'm not here to offer quick fixes or empty promises. Instead, I'm here to provide you with a practical, scientific, and friendly approach to overcoming the relentless mental loop that is overthinking.

But let's start at the beginning. What is overthinking, and why should you care? Picture this: Your mind, a powerful tool, is like a race car that's been revving in the red zone for hours, burning precious mental fuel without ever hitting the track. Overthinking is the act of ruminating on the past, worrying about the future, and dissecting every detail of the present to the point of exhaustion. It's a cognitive treadmill that can leave you feeling drained, anxious, and stuck in a state of analysis paralysis.

Why should we address overthinking at all? Well, imagine all the creative ideas left untapped, the meaningful relationships left unformed, and the opportunities left unexplored—all because our minds were too busy spinning their wheels. Overthinking isn't just an inconvenience; it's a barrier to living our best lives. And that's why I'm passionate about helping you break free from its grip.

Throughout this book, I'll share my own experiences with over-thinking—the sleepless nights, the missed opportunities, and the moments of self-doubt. I want you to know that I'm not just your author; I'm your fellow traveler on this path to mental clarity. My journey with overthinking has shaped my under-standing of the human mind, and it's the driving force behind why I've chosen to delve into this topic.

So, what can you expect from *Help Me Stop Overthinking*? In the following chapters, we'll explore the science behind overthink-ing, the triggers that set it in motion, and the practical strate-gies that can help you regain control of your thoughts. We'll discuss concrete techniques, effective problem-solving methods, and ways to cultivate a more balanced perspective on life. Each section is designed to provide you with actionable insights and practical tools to help you break free from the shackles of overthinking.

But before we dive in, I encourage you to embrace this journey with an open mind and a willingness to change. Overthinking may be a tough nut to crack, but together, we can loosen its grip on your life. So, if you're ready to take the first step toward a more peaceful and purposeful existence, turn the page and let's embark on this transformative adventure together. Your overthinking days are numbered, my friend, and the path to mental freedom starts now.

1

UNDERSTANDING OVERTHINKING

Spend eighty percent of your time focusing on the opportunities of tomorrow rather than the problems of yesterday.

— BRIAN TRACY

I t's time to explore the concept of overthinking in its entirety. Overthinking is a mental process where you excessively dwell on a problem, situation, or decision, often leading to a cycle of negative thoughts and worry. It's like having a thought stuck on replay in your mind, causing unnecessary stress and anxiety. Essentially, it's thinking too much about something to the point where it becomes counterproductive and detrimental to your well-being.

We've all been there, tangled up in the web of our thoughts. But don't worry, we're going to break down this overthinking habit step by step.

You've just written an important email to your colleague, and now you're obsessing over whether you should have used "Regards" or "Sincerely." Your cursor hovers over the send button, and your heart races. Is this email going to change the course of human history? Probably not.

Take a deep breath, hit send, and move on. Remember, people don't analyze your emails as thoroughly as you do. Most of the time, they're just happy to receive a response.

You've been invited to a social gathering, and you're already fretting about who will be there, what you should wear, and whether you'll have anything interesting to say. Remind yourself that everyone else is just as human as you are. They also have their insecurities and fears. Take the pressure off by focusing on being present and genuinely interested in others. Conversations flow when you listen and connect, not when you're planning your next perfect line.

Next, you're faced with a major life decision, and you've created a flowchart, asked your closest friends multiple times, and even asked your neighbor's dog for advice. Research is great, but don't let it become a never-ending quest for the "perfect" answer. Sometimes, you have to trust your gut and make a decision. Not many decisions in life are irreversible.

Do you remember that awkward thing you said three years ago? Yep, it still keeps you up at night. We've all experienced this. Chances are that most people have probably forgotten about it. If it's something you feel the need to say sorry for, do it. Otherwise, forgive yourself and move forward. Remember, you're not defined by your past moments.

Are you constantly worried about what the future holds—career, family, health, and more? Planning is great, but don't try to predict every possible outcome. Focus on what you can control today. Build a strong foundation, and you'll be better prepared for whatever tomorrow brings.

It is now time to look closely at the tangible differences between our regular everyday thinking and overthinking.

- **Quantity vs. quality:** Overthinking involves an excessive amount of thinking, often looping through the same thoughts, whereas regular thinking focuses on a balanced and proportionate analysis of a situation.
- **Emotional impact:** Overthinking tends to be associated with negative emotions like anxiety, stress, and self-doubt. Regular thinking is more balanced and doesn't necessarily lead to overwhelming emotions.

- **Productivity:** Overthinking can be paralyzing and hinder decision-making or problem-solving, while regular thinking is typically more efficient and goal-oriented.
- **Time spent:** Overthinking can consume a significant amount of time and mental energy, while regular thinking is a more streamlined process.
- **Flexibility:** Regular thinking allows for adaptability and the ability to consider various perspectives. Overthinking often fixates on a single viewpoint, making it harder to see the bigger picture.

Remember, it's perfectly normal to think things through and consider your options, but when your thinking patterns become a source of distress and prevent you from moving forward or enjoying the present moment, that's when it's essential to recognize and manage overthinking. You have the capacity to replace your thoughts with more constructive thinking, which can lead to greater peace of mind and better decision-making.

IMPACT OF OVERTHINKING ON MENTAL HEALTH

 Overthinking is the art of creating problems that weren't even there.

— ANONYMOUS

Let's ask ourselves what the impact of overthinking is on mental health and how it can affect your overall well-being. Remember, so many are facing this challenge, and there are ways to manage overthinking and its consequences.

It's important to acknowledge that overthinking can have a profound impact on your mental health. It's like a persistent storm cloud that casts a shadow over your thoughts and emotions. Here are some of the key negative effects:

- **Anxiety:** Overthinking often leads to excessive worrying about future events or past actions. This constant rumination can trigger anxiety, making you feel tense, restless, and overwhelmed. It's like your mind is running a never-ending marathon.
- **Depression:** Over time, the weight of constant negative thoughts and self-criticism can contribute to feelings of hopelessness and sadness. Overthinking can trap you in a cycle of negative thinking, making it difficult to find joy in life.
- **Stress:** The continuous mental chatter can cause chronic stress. Your body stays in a state of heightened alertness, leading to physical symptoms such as headaches, muscle tension, and fatigue.
- **Impaired decision-making:** Overthinking can paralyze your ability to make decisions. You may become indecisive, fearing that every choice will lead to negative outcomes. This can hinder your personal and professional life.

The impact of overthinking can affect both your mind and your body. Here's how:

- **Insomnia:** Racing thoughts can disrupt your sleep patterns. When you're unable to switch off your mind, you might find it difficult to fall asleep or stay asleep, leading to chronic sleep deprivation. This, in turn, can exacerbate mental health issues and weaken your immune system.

- **Weakened immune system:** Chronic stress resulting from overthinking can weaken your immune system. Stress hormones like cortisol can compromise your body's ability to fight off infections and diseases.
- **Digestive problems:** Stress and anxiety from overthinking can impact your digestive system, leading to issues such as irritable bowel syndrome (IBS), indigestion, and nausea.
- **Cardiovascular issues:** Prolonged stress can contribute to high blood pressure, heart disease, and other cardiovascular problems, putting your physical health at risk.

If you find yourself trapped in the cycle of overthinking, please know that you can take steps to regain control over your thoughts and emotions:

- **Seek professional help:** A therapist or counselor can provide guidance and techniques to manage overthinking, anxiety, and depression effectively.
- **Set realistic goals:** Break down tasks into manageable steps and avoid the paralysis of indecision. Celebrate your achievements, no matter how small.
- **Self-compassion:** Be kind to yourself. Replace self-criticism with self-compassion. Remember that you're human, and you are not expected to be perfect.
- **Healthy lifestyle:** Prioritize good sleep, exercise, and a balanced diet. These practices can significantly improve both mental and physical health.

You have the strength to overcome the challenges of overthinking. Seek support when needed and take small steps toward a healthier and more peaceful mind. Your mental and physical well-being are worth the effort, and there's a brighter future ahead of you.

Ask yourself, "Have I ever wondered why overthinking happens?" Overthinking is a common experience, and it's crucial to recognize that you're not in this struggle by yourself. Together, we'll explore the intricate web of factors contributing to overthinking, the triggers that set it in motion, and the role your brain plays in this mental process.

- **Personality traits**: Some individuals are naturally inclined to overthink due to their personality traits. For instance, people with high levels of neuroticism tend to ruminate more, pondering over perceived threats or negative outcomes. These traits can make them more susceptible to overthinking.
- **Past experiences:** Our past experiences significantly shape our thought patterns. Traumatic events, especially, can become a breeding ground for overthinking. The mind revisits these events, seeking understanding, resolution, or avoidance, often leading to a cycle of persistent thoughts.
- **Cognitive biases:** Your brain has a remarkable ability to process information efficiently. However, this efficiency can backfire when it falls prey to cognitive biases. Confirmation bias, for example, causes you to

focus on information that confirms your existing beliefs, reinforcing your overthinking loop.

Below, we will investigate some of the most common triggers for people when faced with overthinking:

- **Uncertainty:** When faced with uncertain situations, the brain tends to engage in excessive analysis to mitigate perceived risks. Overthinking, in this context, is an attempt to regain a sense of control.
- **Perfectionism:** Striving for perfection can fuel overthinking. The fear of making mistakes or not meeting self-imposed standards can lead to incessant rumination on tasks and decisions.
- **Social comparison:** Comparing yourself to others can trigger overthinking about your worth, accomplishments, and appearance, often resulting in feelings of inadequacy or jealousy.
- **Rumination:** Dwelling on past mistakes or negative events, without constructive problem-solving, can lead to a cycle of overthinking that hinders personal growth.

The human brain exhibits remarkable complexity, albeit accompanied by idiosyncrasies. Among its intricate neural networks, the default mode network (DMN) assumes the role of orchestrating spontaneous and self-referential cognitive processes. This network becomes engaged during periods of mental introspection, a propensity that frequently underlies the phenomenon of excessive rumination (Editors of Psychology Today, 2021).

From a historical perspective, this function might have provided benefits for planning, decision-making, and problem-solving. Nonetheless, in today's society, it can become a hindrance, resulting in cyclic and unproductive thoughts often linked with overthinking.

Your brain is like a supercomputer, processing an incredible amount of information every second. Sometimes, it gets a little carried away, like a car spinning its wheels in the mud. But the good news is that you can regain control over those racing thoughts.

It's important to realize that you're not a prisoner of your past experiences, personality traits, or cognitive biases. You have the power to change these patterns, and it all starts with awareness and self-compassion.

One effective way to combat overthinking is through professional therapy. A trained therapist can help you navigate your thoughts and equip you with the tools to manage them. It's like having a personal guide through the jungle of your mind.

Cognitive restructuring is another handy technique. It's like reprogramming your brain's software. The idea is to notice the negative thoughts and replace them with more positive ones. Sounds simple, but it takes practice.

Problem-solving techniques are also in our toolkit. They help you break down complex issues into manageable pieces and tackle them one by one. It's like taking a big, overwhelming puzzle and working on one piece at a time.

We also need to explore the concept of productive and unproductive thinking. These aren't just fancy terms; they're vital to your mental well-being.

Productive thinking is the hero of the story. It's creative, solution-oriented, adaptable, and goal-oriented. Imagine it as your trusty sidekick, always ready to help you conquer challenges and achieve your goals.

On the flip side, unproductive thinking is like the villain that sneaks into your thoughts when you least expect it. It leads to rumination, negative emotions, inertia, closed-mindedness, and distraction. Recognizing it is the first step in defeating it.

Why should you care about this distinction? Because productive thinking brings a slew of benefits to the table. It's like the golden ticket to a better life.

Effective problem-solving is one of its benefits. It helps you identify and solve problems, paving the way for personal and professional success. Imagine being the private investigator of your own life.

It also fuels innovation and creativity. If you want to come up with brilliant ideas and approaches, productive thinking is your ally.

And don't forget about your emotional well-being. Productive thinking is linked to lower stress levels and improved mental health. It's your path to a more positive outlook on life.

Plus, it makes you adaptable, so you can roll with the punches that life throws your way. And guess what? It boosts your productivity by helping you make the most of your time and resources.

But beware of the dangers of unproductive thinking. It can lead to mental health issues, impaired decision-making, stagnation, interpersonal conflicts, and missed opportunities. Nobody wants that, right?

So, here's the bottom line: You have the power to change your thought patterns, and understanding the difference between productive and unproductive thinking is your secret weapon. Armed with this knowledge, you can take control of your thoughts, reduce overthinking, and live a more empowered, present, and fulfilled life. You've got this!

In summary, productive thinking is characterized by a solution-oriented, positive mindset, whereas unproductive thinking tends to involve rumination, negativity, and stagnation. Cultivating productive thinking can lead to improved problem-solving, creativity, mental health, and overall well-being, while avoiding the pitfalls of unproductive thinking is crucial for personal and professional development. Scientific research supports the idea that our thought patterns can significantly impact our cognitive and emotional health, making it essential to nurture productive thinking habits (BC Campus, 2014).

THE ACTION STEPS

In our journey toward overcoming overthinking and managing worries effectively, let's explore two crucial action steps that can make a significant difference in your life.

Begin by taking a closer look at your own thinking patterns. Often, overthinking can be so ingrained in our daily lives that we don't even realize we're doing it. I encourage you to set aside some time for self-reflection. I have given you a few suggestions to get you started:

- Can you reflect on a recent situation where you were overthinking? What triggered this overthinking episode?
- How did this excessive thinking impact your mood or behavior?
- Are there recurring themes or specific situations that tend to lead to overthinking?

Consider keeping a journal or a notebook handy to jot down your thoughts and responses to these questions. This process will help you become more aware of when and why you tend to overthink, which is the first step toward taking control.

Creating a Worry List

Worries and concerns are a natural part of life, but they can become overwhelming if left unorganized. To regain control, start by creating a worry list. Here's how:

- Take a moment to write down all the worries and concerns that are currently on your mind. Don't hold back; list everything, big or small.
- Once you've compiled your list, review it carefully. Now, prioritize these worries based on their level of

importance. Consider factors like urgency, impact on your life, and how much control you have over them.

- Assign a number or ranking to each worry to indicate its priority. For instance, you can use a scale from 1–10, with one being the least important and ten being the most crucial.

By creating this worry list and assigning priorities, you'll gain clarity on what truly deserves your attention and energy. This method prevents you from getting bogged down by less important concerns and allows you to focus on addressing the most significant issues in your life.

In this chapter, we've looked deep into the intricate web of overthinking, exploring its various manifestations, triggers, and consequences. We've witnessed how overthinking can act as a relentless companion, hijacking our thoughts and steering us away from clarity. Now, as we transition into the next chapter, we'll venture into the realm of science to unravel the fascinating intricacies of overthinking. By understanding the underlying mechanisms and neural pathways that contribute to this common human experience, we aim to empower ourselves with the knowledge necessary to break free from the clutches of overthinking and regain control over our minds. So, let's embark on this scientific journey, armed with curiosity and the determination to unlock the secrets of overthinking.

2

THE SCIENCE OF OVERTHINKING

 When opportunity knocks, overthinking can cause the door to slam shut.

— ANONYMOUS

Welcome to a new chapter in our voyage through the mind. In this chapter, we will embark on a fascinating exploration of the intricate science behind a common human experience: overthinking. Prepare to delve deep into the inner workings of our brains as we unravel the complex neural processes and cognitive biases that underlie this pervasive phenomenon. We'll also shine a spotlight on the profound impact of stress and anxiety, two formidable foes of clear thinking, as we navigate the treacherous waters of overthinking. To set the stage for our exploration, consider this thought-provoking statistic: Studies show that 73% of people experience overthinking on a regular basis, making it a ubiquitous challenge in our modern lives (Acosta, 2022). So fasten your intellectual seatbelt and get ready to journey into the fascinating world of overthinking.

Today, I'd like to take you through the intricate landscape of the human brain and explore the fascinating world of overthinking. We'll explore the various brain processes at play, backed by scientific evidence, to help you understand why overthinking can be such a persistent and sometimes troublesome mental habit.

Let's begin by introducing you to the key players in our brain's drama of overthinking: the prefrontal cortex, the amygdala, and the hippocampus.

- **Prefrontal cortex:** This brain region, often considered the "thinking" part of the brain, resides in the frontal lobe. It's responsible for complex cognitive behavior, decision-making, personality expression, and moderating social behavior. When it comes to overthinking, the prefrontal cortex plays a pivotal role. It's the part responsible for generating and evaluating thoughts, including those that lead to excessive rumination and worry (Potts, 2019).
- **Amygdala:** Deep within our brain's temporal lobe, the amygdala takes the spotlight. This almond-shaped structure is an emotional powerhouse. It processes emotions and is particularly sensitive to fear and stress. When we overthink, the amygdala can become overactive, heightening our emotional responses, and triggering a cascade of anxious thoughts (Potts, 2019).

- **Hippocampus:** Situated near the amygdala, the hippocampus is a critical player in memory formation and consolidation. Overthinking involves revisiting past events, reevaluating decisions, or worrying about the future. The hippocampus is responsible for retrieving relevant memories, making it a central component of the overthinking process (Potts, 2019).

Overthinking can unlock the hidden chambers of our mind, revealing insights we never knew were there, but it's a double-edged sword that can also lead to the path of doubt.

— ANONYMOUS

How do our brain regions team up in the overthinking process? Picture it as a dynamic orchestra of thoughts and emotions, all playing their part in the symphony of your mind.

When you're faced with a tough decision or a challenging situation, your prefrontal cortex takes the stage. It's like the conductor, generating thoughts and possible scenarios. If that situation triggers fear or stress—cue the amygdala—your prefrontal cortex can go into overdrive. It starts belting out an entire concerto of worst-case scenarios, and suddenly, you're trapped in an endless loop of analysis paralysis.

The hippocampus, your brain's resident librarian, jumps into action. It starts flipping through the pages of your memory, pulling out past experiences and memories that might be relevant to the current situation. Now, you're not just stuck in the present; you're dissecting and replaying past events in your mind, too.

And then there's the DMN, the daydreamer of your brain. This network of brain regions becomes active when you're not laser-focused on a specific task or the outside world. Instead, it turns inward, leading to self-reflection and mind-wandering. Think of it as your brain's internal television, constantly playing reruns of your thoughts.

The DMN can be a double-edged sword. It's fantastic for creative thinking and introspection, but it can also fuel overthinking. When it goes into overdrive, it can create a never-ending loop of self-criticism, rumination, and excessive worrying.

Neuroimaging studies using techniques like functional MRI (fMRI) have actually shown that overthinking is associated with increased brain activity in the regions we've been talking about—the prefrontal cortex, amygdala, and hippocampus. It's like they light up like a neon sign when we overthink (Potts, 2019).

Chronic overthinking isn't just a harmless mental gymnastics routine. It's like a heavyweight champion that can pack a punch to your brain. Studies have found that it can lead to decreased gray matter density in the prefrontal cortex, which can impair your cognitive function and even increase the risk of mental health issues like anxiety and depression (Millson, 2022).

What you're experiencing isn't just in your head; it's backed by solid scientific evidence. Understanding the roles of the prefrontal cortex, amygdala, hippocampus, and the DMN can shine a light on why your mind sometimes gets caught in these endless loops of thought. But don't despair; armed with this knowledge, you've got the power to break free and start managing and mitigating the effects of overthinking on your mental well-being.

COGNITIVE BIASES AND OVERTHINKING

Let's start things off by exploring three common cognitive biases: confirmation bias, availability bias, and negativity bias. These sneaky mental habits can lead us down the overthinking rabbit hole faster than you can say, "I should stop thinking so much!"

Confirmation bias is like a loyal sidekick to our preconceived notions. It makes us seek out information that aligns with our beliefs, while conveniently ignoring anything that challenges our views. So, if you've ever found yourself deep in a political debate, only reading articles that echo your own opinions, you're in the confirmation bias club.

Availability bias, on the other hand, tricks us into believing that recent or easily recalled information is the be-all and end-all. Remember that rare plane crash you heard about on the news? It might make you think twice about flying, even though statistically, it's safer than crossing the street. Availability bias thrives on sensational stories and anecdotal evidence, leading us to overthink decisions.

Lastly, negativity bias, our ancient survival instinct, makes us give more weight to negative experiences than positive ones. While it helped our ancestors stay alert to potential threats, it can make us obsess over criticism or negative feedback, fueling the fires of overthinking.

How can we make these biases feel a bit more relatable? Can you imagine yourself in a heated debate with a friend who has opposing political views? You dive into your trusted echo chamber of news articles that align with your beliefs, thinking you're well-informed. As the conversation continues, you begin to realize that you made a choice to inform yourself of all sides. Little do you know; you're falling right into the confirmation bias trap.

Or imagine you're contemplating a career change after hearing about your friend's high-paying gig in a new field. Instead of considering that your friend might be a rare exception, you're ready to dive in, ignoring the competitive job market. That's availability bias in action.

Now, let's not forget negativity bias. You've just received a glowing performance review with one tiny criticism. Instead of basking in your achievements, you fixate on that one negative comment, spiraling into unnecessary self-doubt and overthinking. You keep yourself awake at night, reviewing the many years you have spent with this company and all you have done wrong. You worry about what your superiors actually think of your work.

Understanding these cognitive biases is important because they're like the secret architects of our overthinking tendencies. But fear not because knowledge is power, my friend. By recognizing these biases when they pop up, questioning your thought processes, and seeking out balanced information, you can break free from the chains of overthinking.

We can't forget that stress and anxiety are like the sneakier, subtler villains in our story. They don't just mess with our emotions; they mess with our heads too.

When stress and anxiety enter the scene, they trigger a cascade of neurobiological responses. Cortisol, the stress hormone, gets released, preparing us to face the perceived threat. In small doses, this is helpful, but chronic stress can mess with your cognitive mojo.

The sympathetic nervous system, or the "fight or flight" system, also gets into action. Your heart races, your breathing becomes shallow, and you're on high alert. This heightened state of hypervigilance is a prime breeding ground for overthinking.

In the long run, chronic stress keeps your brain in a state of hyperarousal. You end up overthinking everything, from problems to worries to perceived threats. It's like your brain is stuck on a never-ending thought treadmill.

Anxiety brings its own weapon to the party: rumination. It's like a broken record, replaying your worries and fears over and over again. Chronic rumination is a hallmark of anxiety disorders and a surefire way to exacerbate overthinking tendencies.

There are ways to beat this overthinking villainy.

 CBT therapy: The compass that guides the lost ship of overthinking back to the shores of clarity.

— ANONYMOUS

At its core, cognitive behavioral therapy is a type of psychotherapy or talk therapy that focuses on the connection between our thoughts, feelings, and behaviors. It's based on the idea that the way we think about things can influence how we feel and what we do. In the context of overthinking, CBT helps you recognize and change those unhelpful thinking patterns that keep you stuck in the overthinking loop.

CBT starts by helping you become more aware of your thought patterns. It encourages you to pay close attention to the thoughts that trigger your overthinking episodes. This is detective work, where you uncover the culprits behind your mental distress.

Once you've identified these thoughts, CBT helps you challenge their accuracy and validity. It asks you to question whether your thoughts are based on evidence or if they're distorted by cognitive biases. By doing this, you begin to separate rational concerns from irrational fears.

CBT then guides you to reframe your thoughts in a more balanced and constructive way. This is where you replace those overbearing, negative thoughts with more realistic and positive ones. It's like swapping out a gloomy painting for a vibrant one in the gallery of your mind.

It equips you with practical tools and coping strategies to manage overthinking. These could include relaxation techniques, mindfulness exercises, or problem-solving skills. These tools give you the power to respond to overthinking episodes with healthier, more adaptive responses.

This type of therapy often involves setting specific goals and assigning homework between sessions. This homework might include practicing new thought patterns, monitoring your thoughts, or implementing relaxation exercises. It's like a workout routine for your mind, helping you build mental resilience.

Throughout your CBT journey, you'll track your progress. You'll notice how your thinking patterns, emotions, and behaviors evolve over time. This self-reflection can be quite enlightening, as it helps you see the tangible results of your efforts.

We should ask why CBT works for overthinkers?

It directly addresses the distorted thinking patterns that fuel overthinking. By teaching you to challenge and reframe your thoughts, it puts you in control of your mental narrative. It is so effective because it is one of the most extensively researched and evidence-based therapies out there. Numerous studies have shown its effectiveness in treating various mental health issues, including overthinking and anxiety (Hofmann et al., 2012).

CBT doesn't just dwell on theory; it gives you actionable strategies that you can use in your daily life. These tools empower you to respond differently to overthinking triggers. It is a working relationship with you and your therapist. You actively participate in setting goals, challenging your thoughts, and working on strategies. This partnership is key to its success.

CBT isn't about dwelling on past traumas or problems; it's about finding solutions and moving forward. It's future-oriented and emphasizes building a toolkit for managing future challenges.

In essence, CBT is like a mentor for your mind, guiding you toward healthier thought patterns and behaviors. It's a practical, action-oriented approach that can help you break free from the grip of overthinking and lead a more balanced and peaceful life.

Lifestyle factors play a part too. Getting enough sleep, regular exercise, and maintaining a balanced diet can boost your resilience to stress and anxiety, giving your cognitive functions a fighting chance.

Chronic stress can leave your working memory in shambles, making it tough to focus and contributing to cognitive overload. You end up second-guessing everything and, you guessed it, overthinking your choices. Under stress, you're more likely to make impulsive or overly cautious decisions. It's like a tug-of-war between your instincts and your rational mind, leaving you in a decision-making dilemma.

In a nutshell, the effects of stress and anxiety on overthinking are complex and deeply rooted in our biology. But don't let that discourage you! By understanding these mechanisms, you're already ahead of the game. With the right stress management techniques and therapeutic interventions, you can beat the overthinking blues and reclaim your mental clarity.

Take a deep breath and know that you have the tools to tackle overthinking head-on. You're not alone in this journey; we're all in the same boat, grappling with these biases and battling stress. Embrace the knowledge and remember that a little less overthinking leads to a lot more peace of mind. Here's to a brighter, less cluttered, and more focused future!

THE ACTION STEPS

Let's discuss the action steps for identifying and addressing common cognitive distortions, the impact of stress on over-thinking, and the exercises to help you manage these cognitive biases.

Action steps for identifying and addressing cognitive distortions.

The first step is to become aware of your thought patterns. Pay close attention to your inner dialogue and emotional reactions. Scientifically, cognitive distortions are biased ways of thinking that can lead to negative emotions and behaviors.

Look for frequent cognitive distortions in your thinking. Here are three examples:

- **All-or-nothing thinking:** Viewing situations in extreme terms, such as success or failure, with no middle ground. An example: "I made one mistake at work; I'm a total failure."
- **Catastrophizing:** Assuming the worst possible outcome will occur. An example: "If I don't get this job, my life is over."
- **Mind reading:** This happens when you feel others are thinking and assuming negatively. An example: "They didn't invite me; they must not like me."

Once you've identified a cognitive distortion, challenge it with evidence and reframe the thought in a more balanced way. Ask yourself:

- "Can I support this thought?"
- "Am I making assumptions without facts?"
- "What's a more realistic way to view this situation?"

Confirmation bias is the tendency to seek information that confirms pre-existing beliefs. To combat this, encourage yourself to:

- Choose a belief or opinion you strongly hold.
- Seek out information that contradicts this belief.
- Reflect on how this new information impacts your perspective.

Stress can exacerbate overthinking by overwhelming the mind with worry and anxiety. To help understand this impact, I have provided prompts for journaling or reflection:

- **Journaling prompt:** Think about a time when you were under a lot of stress:

  ○ How did it impact your thinking?
  ○ Did you find yourself overthinking more than usual?
  ○ Describe your thoughts, emotions, and behaviors during that stressful period. This reflection can help you recognize the connection between stress and overthinking.

In summary, addressing cognitive distortions requires self-awareness, identification, and the application of cognitive restructuring techniques. Stress management is vital to preventing overthinking, and these exercises can be effective tools in this process. I encourage you to practice these steps consistently to promote healthier thought patterns and reduce overthinking.

As we delve deeper into the intricate science of overthinking, it becomes evident that this mental labyrinth holds many secrets waiting to be unraveled. The preceding chapter has shed light on the complexities of our thoughts, the neural pathways that can lead us astray, and the detrimental effects of chronic rumination. Now, armed with a deeper understanding of the problem, we are poised to explore the solutions. In the upcoming chapter, we will embark on a voyage through a myriad of practical strategies and techniques designed to help you overcome the clutches of overthinking. So, as we turn the page, let's prepare to navigate the maze of our minds with purpose, forging a path toward greater clarity, peace, and productivity.

3

STRATEGIES TO OVERCOME OVERTHINKING

 People become attached to their burdens sometimes more than the burdens are attached to them.

— GEORGE BERNARD SHAW

I t's late at night, and you're nestled under your blankets, but instead of drifting off into dreamland, your brain decides to put on a one-person show. It replays every conversation you had during the day, frets about what tomorrow holds, and jumps into the mysteries of the universe, all while the clock keeps ticking away. It's like an Oscar-worthy performance, and you, my friend, are stuck in the audience, unable to yell, "Cut!"

Overthinking is like that friend who shows up uninvited and overstays their welcome. But I've got some practical tools, strategies, and relatable stories to help you break free from this overthinking prison.

In this chapter, we're going to explore some down-to-earth, scientifically-backed techniques. Hang in there with me because there's always more to learn, more to try, and definitely more hope to be found.

Let's paint a different picture for a moment: You're driving down a bustling street during rush hour. The traffic is pure chaos, horns are blaring left and right, and your mind is doing its usual marathon of work, errands, and deadlines. Sound all too familiar? We've all been there, stuck in that blur of thoughts and distractions, and it feels like there's no way out.

But trust me, there is a way out, and together, we're going to find it. So, buckle up because this journey to stop overthinking is going to be a whole lot more exciting than rush hour traffic!

ERIN'S STORY

A few years ago, Erin found herself constantly overwhelmed by the demands of daily life. Her mind was a never-ending tornado of worries and to-do lists. She felt like she was living on autopilot, just going through the motions. She knew something had to change.

Ask yourself, have you ever felt like you're just mindlessly moving through life like it is passing you by without really experiencing it?

That's where mindfulness comes into play. It's not some mystical concept or a far-out practice. Mindfulness is simply the art of being present and fully engaged in the here and now. It's about taking a step back from the chaos and finding clarity in the present moment.

Do you find yourself constantly dwelling on the past or worrying about the future? What impact does this have on your daily life?

Mindfulness offers a way out of this cycle. When we use this, we can be more cognizant of our thoughts and feelings without judgment. Think of it as putting a spotlight on your inner world. When you shine that light, you start to see things more clearly.

Can you recall a recent moment when you were fully present and engaged in what you were doing? How did it make you feel?

Meet Tom, a devoted father and husband who, for years, carried the weight of the world on his shoulders. Work deadlines, family responsibilities, and friendship obligations constantly swirled in his mind, leaving him overwhelmed and drained. Tom's overthinking tendencies not only stole his sleep but also robbed him of the simple pleasure of enjoying a meal.

Tom's turning point came when he stumbled upon some scientific research about mindfulness. He realized that his constant mental chatter was causing him more harm than good. It was time to make a change.

As he explored the world of mindfulness, Tom found practical suggestions that spoke to him. He began with a simple daily routine: Setting aside a few minutes each morning to focus on his breath. At first, it was a struggle. His mind would wander to work, family, and everything in between. But Tom persevered.

Gradually, Tom started to notice a shift. His thoughts became less chaotic, and he learned to be more intentional with his actions. Instead of juggling tasks haphazardly, he began to prioritize and tackle them one at a time. Work became more manageable, and he felt more present with his family and friends.

Sure, there were days when Tom still found himself slipping into old habits of overthinking. But now, armed with mindfulness techniques, he knew how to gently guide his thoughts back to the present moment. He was learning to balance his responsibilities without losing himself in the process.

Tom's journey was not always smooth sailing, but he found relief in the simplicity of mindfulness. He realized that by being kinder to himself and staying present, he could navigate the complexities of life with a newfound sense of ease and joy.

Now, let's get practical. How can you bring mindfulness into your life? Well, it's all about small steps. Here are a few techniques that have worked for many:

- **Body scans:** Imagine you're lying down, and you mentally scan your body from head to toe, noticing any tension or discomfort. Focus on trying to release any tension you may feel. This simple exercise can help you release physical stress and connect with your body.
- **Sensory awareness:** Engage your senses. Take a moment to truly taste your food, feel the texture of an object in your hand, or listen to the sounds around you. It's incredible how much we miss when we're not paying attention. How often do you eat without really savoring the flavors or walk through a park without appreciating the beauty of nature?
- **Mindful walking:** The next time you're strolling down the street, pay attention to each step and the sensation of your feet hitting the ground. It's a simple way to anchor yourself in the present.
- **Mindful eating:** Have you ever devoured a meal in front of the TV, hardly aware of what you were eating? Mindful eating is about savoring each bite, truly tasting your food, and appreciating the nourishment it

provides. Do you often multitask while eating, and does this affect your relationship with food?

These mindfulness techniques are like tools in your mental toolbox. You can use them whenever you need a moment of clarity and presence in your day. So ask yourself, "Am I willing to give mindfulness a try, even if it seems unfamiliar or challenging?"

And here's the real truth behind mindfulness—it's not just about being present. It's about becoming more mindful of the actions we take in life. In chapter six, we'll delve deeper into how mindfulness can help you set meaningful goals and pursue the life you truly desire. We'll talk about how taking small amounts of time to think and write out your goals can be a game-changer.

You know those moments when your mind feels like a runaway train, endlessly circling the same worries and doubts? Yeah, we've all been there. But what if I told you there's a way to hop off that mental treadmill and find some clarity? It's called Cognitive Behavioral Therapy (CBT), and trust me, it's a game-changer.

Let me share a story about Sarah. She used to be the queen of overthinking. Every decision, big or small, felt like a life-altering choice. One day, she stumbled upon CBT. It was like a lightbulb moment. She learned that her thoughts were driving her anxiety, and CBT could help her regain control. Have you ever felt like Sarah, stuck in a never-ending cycle of worrying about the future or dwelling on past mistakes?

As we discussed earlier, CBT is like a map for your mind. It helps you navigate those winding roads of thoughts and feelings. Essentially, it's all about recognizing that your thoughts influence your emotions and behaviors. If you can manage to change your thoughts, you can change your world.

Meet Alex. He was his own worst critic, constantly beating himself up over perceived failures. With CBT, Alex started practicing something called "cognitive restructuring." This fancy term simply means challenging negative thoughts and replacing them with more balanced ones. Do you ever catch yourself in a cycle of self-criticism, where your inner voice becomes your harshest judge?

I want you to think of cognitive restructuring as a mental makeover. You take those negative thoughts and put them under the microscope. Ask yourself, "Is this thought based on facts, or am I jumping to conclusions?"

Now, let me introduce you to Mike. He used to avoid social gatherings and opportunities because he was afraid of rejection. But with CBT's "behavioral activation" technique, he started gradually facing his fears. Each step outside his comfort zone was like a victory. Have you ever missed out on something great because you were too afraid to step out of your comfort zone?

Behavioral activation is like a fitness routine for your mental health. You start small and work your way up. Each time you confront a fear or do something you've been avoiding, you're strengthening your resilience.

PRACTICAL EXERCISES

Now, here's where things get hands-on. CBT offers practical exercises like "thought records" and "behavior experiments." These tools help you gather evidence about your thoughts and behaviors, much like a detective solving a case. If I told you that by jotting down your thoughts and tracking your actions, you could gain valuable insights into your overthinking patterns, would you give it a try?

- **Thought records:** Imagine a thought record as your mental notepad. You jot down the situation, your automatic thoughts, emotions, and evidence that supports or refutes those thoughts. It's like unraveling your mind.
- **Behavior experiments:** Think of behavior experiments as real-life trials. You test your assumptions by doing things you'd typically avoid and observe what happens. It's like conducting scientific experiments on your own life.

JOURNALING

 Journaling: The art of untangling the web of overthinking, one pen stroke at a time.

— ANONYMOUS

Imagine a crowded intersection in the heart of a bustling city. People rush by, each lost in their own thoughts, distracted by the daily activities of life. In the midst of this chaos, there's a person standing still, a journal in hand, jotting down their thoughts. This person is you, and your journal is your sanctuary, a place where the noise of the world gives way to the clarity of your own mind.

Our minds are like the aforementioned bustling city intersection, with thoughts racing in every direction. Overthinking becomes our default mode, causing stress, anxiety, and a sense of being overwhelmed.

But here's the thing: Just as that person found solace in the journal amidst the chaos, you can find tranquility in journaling too. It's not about solving all your problems with a pen and paper, but it's about untangling the knots in your mind and gaining valuable insights into your own thought patterns.

Think about a time when you found yourself upset, anxious, or stressed without fully understanding why. It's a common experience, right? Now, let's pose a thought-provoking question: How can you tackle an issue if you can't even identify what's causing it?

This is where journaling can be your saving grace. By putting your thoughts on paper, you externalize your inner world. You begin to see patterns, triggers, and recurring themes. You might discover that you're most anxious after interacting with a certain person or that stress creeps in when you procrastinate. This self-awareness can be the beginning of change for you.

Imagine you're trying to solve a puzzle, but the pieces are scattered and you don't even know what the final picture looks like. Overthinking can feel just like that. But with journaling, you start gathering those puzzle pieces.

You jot down your thoughts when you're feeling overwhelmed, and slowly, you begin to see connections. "Ah, every time I have a tight deadline, I become a bundle of nerves," you realize. That's a trigger, and recognizing it is a game-changer. Once you know your triggers, you can prepare for them, develop coping strategies, or even avoid them when possible.

PRACTICAL EXERCISES FOR YOUR JOURNAL

Now, if you're thinking, "Okay, journaling sounds nice, but where do I start?" Don't worry; many others feel the same way. Here are a few "if" statements for you:

- If you're unsure what to write, start with a simple daily log. Jot down your feelings, events, and any notable thoughts at the end of each day.
- If you want to dive deeper, use prompts. For instance, "What am I grateful for today?" or "What's one challenge I faced, and how did I handle it?"
- If you're concerned about privacy, remember that your journal is for your eyes only. It's a judgment-free zone.
- If you're worried about consistency, set a timer for just five minutes each day to write. You'll be surprised at how it becomes a habit.
- If you're skeptical about the benefits, remember that scientific research backs this up. Studies show that journaling can reduce stress, improve mood, and boost overall well-being (WebMD Editors, 2021).

So, does journaling sound too good to be true? Well, consider this: It's a simple yet powerful tool that has helped countless individuals gain clarity, reduce overthinking, and take control of their lives.

In conclusion, I'm not here to lecture you but to share a conversation about a practice that has made a real difference in many lives. It's about embracing the chaos of your mind and finding order through the written word. So, if you're still on the fence about journaling, give it a try. If this is something new for you, consider trying it once a week for a month and see how you feel. Do you feel better? Do you feel like your thoughts are more manageable?

You might just discover the clarity and peace you've been seeking.

PROGRESSIVE MUSCLE RELAXATION

I want you to imagine you're standing in front of a crowded room, about to give a speech. Your heart races, your palms are sweaty, and it feels like a herd of wild horses are stampeding through your chest. It's a scenario that many of us have faced at some point in our lives, and it's a prime example of how stress and anxiety can take hold of us when we least expect it.

Now, let's take a moment to step back and consider a different scenario. You're sitting in a comfortable chair, and you've just finished a session of Progressive Muscle Relaxation (PMR). Your body feels like a warm, relaxed puddle of contentment. The tension that once gripped your muscles has melted away, leaving you with a sense of calm and tranquility.

The difference between these two scenarios is not just a matter of luck or circumstance. It's a testament to the power of PMR, a simple yet highly effective technique for reducing stress and anxiety.

Progressive Muscle Relaxation is like a kick start for your body and mind. It's an approach involving the cycle of tensing and then relaxing your muscle groups allowing the release of physical and mental tension.

Let's take a moment to relate this to a common experience we all share: the stress of rushing through a hectic day. You know those moments when you're stuck in traffic, deadlines are looming, and it feels like the world is closing in on you? Your muscles tighten, your jaw clenches, and your shoulders creep up to your ears. It's as if your body is preparing for a battle that isn't there.

Now, consider this: What if you could release that tension, like a valve letting out steam from a pressure cooker? That's precisely what PMR allows you to do.

Meet Kristen, a dedicated teacher who had a heart as big as her classroom. She was a chronic overthinker, always worrying that she wasn't doing enough for her students. This self-imposed pressure soon trickled into her belief that she wasn't doing enough for her family, friends, and, most importantly, herself.

The weight of these thoughts became unbearable, and Kristen sought help from a therapist. Her therapist introduced her to a practical technique called Progressive Muscle Relaxation. It was exactly what she needed.

Whenever Kristen found herself spiraling into a whirlpool of overthinking, she remembered her therapist's advice. She started clenching and releasing her muscles with intention. As she did so, she focused on her breath and let go of the tension that had gripped her for so long.

It wasn't an instant fix, but over time, Kristen began to notice a difference. The physical act of relaxing her muscles became a powerful tool to quiet her racing thoughts. It was like hitting the reset button on her anxious mind.

As Kristen practiced PMR, she realized that she didn't have to carry the weight of the world on her shoulders. She could still be a dedicated teacher, a loving family member, and a supportive friend without losing herself in the process.

Sure, there were moments when doubts crept in, but had a newfound tool to combat them. She was regaining her sense of peace, one muscle at a time. Kristen"s journey was proof that small, practical changes could lead to significant relief. She was learning that taking care of herself was not a selfish act but a necessary one, allowing her to be the best version of herself for those she cared about most.

Before we dive into how to practice PMR, let's explore why you should give it a try. Imagine these benefits becoming part of your daily life:

- **Stress reduction:** PMR is a proven stress-buster. By systematically relaxing your muscles, you're signaling to your brain that it's time to calm down. The result? Reduced stress and anxiety levels.
- **Improved sleep:** If you've ever tossed and turned at night, your mind racing with worries, PMR can be your

ticket to dreamland. Relaxing your body before bed can lead to more restful and rejuvenating sleep.

- **Enhanced focus:** Picture this: a cluttered desk, a never-ending to-do list, and a mind that's all over the place. PMR can help you regain your focus by clearing away mental cobwebs and distractions.
- **Physical comfort:** Those persistent headaches, backaches, and shoulder knots? PMR can provide relief by addressing the physical tension that often accompanies stress.

How do you actually do Progressive Muscle Relaxation? It's simpler than you might think. Here's a step-by-step guide:

- **Step 1: Find your sanctuary:** Finding the perfect place for your PMR session is key. Consider creating a calming ambiance in this space. Dim the lights, add some soothing music or nature sounds, and perhaps even use essential oils like lavender for added relaxation.
- **Step 2: Get comfy:** Beyond comfortable clothing, try using a soft blanket or cushion to enhance your comfort. Ensure complete disconnection from the outside world by using earplugs or an eye mask, if needed. This step is about creating a cocoon of serenity.
- **Step 3: Breathe in, breathe out:** Take your breathwork to the next level by practicing mindfulness with your breathing. As you inhale, imagine drawing in the stressors of the day, and as you exhale, visualize releasing that stress and tension. Focus on the

sensation of your breath filling your lungs and leaving your body.

- **Step 4: The progressive part:** Let's add mental imagery to enhance this technique. As you tense each muscle group, visualize the tension like a ball of stress or a dark cloud gathering in that area. Imagine a warm, soothing color like a golden light or calming blue washing over the relaxed muscles as you release the tension. Visualize this color spreading a sense of calm and comfort. As you release each muscle group, silently repeat a positive affirmation related to that area. For example, as you release your neck and shoulders, you might affirm, "I am letting go of tension and embracing relaxation." Here's a suggested sequence:

  - toes and feet
  - calves and shins
  - thighs and buttocks
  - abdomen
  - chest and upper back
  - hands and arms
  - neck and shoulders
  - face—yes, even your facial muscles can hold tension

- **Step 5: Include your senses:** Engage multiple senses during your PMR session. Light a scented candle or use an essential oil diffuser with a calming scent like chamomile or sandalwood. Play soft, soothing music or nature sounds. During muscle tensing, gently press your fingers against the tensed muscles. As you release, notice the vast difference in sensations between tension and relaxation.

- **Step 6: Smile and express gratitude:** End your PMR session with a smile and a moment of gratitude. Reflect on the peace and relaxation you've just experienced. Give thanks for this time you've dedicated to self-care.
- **Step 7: Transition mindfully:** As you transition back to your daily routine, do so mindfully. Carry the sense of calm with you. Consider making a cup of herbal tea or engaging in a brief grounding exercise to maintain the peaceful feeling you've cultivated.

By adding these elements and expanding on the original steps, you can create a more enriching and unique Progressive Muscle Relaxation experience, making it an even more powerful tool in your journey toward reducing overthinking and finding inner peace.

If you're feeling stressed, anxious, or overwhelmed, taking just 10–15 minutes each day for PMR can actually save you time and energy in the long run. It's an investment in your well-being that pays dividends.

If you're thinking to yourself, "I've heard this before," that is understandable. Many have heard of PMR but never tried it. So, why not give it a shot? The benefits are real, and it doesn't require any special equipment or training.

PMR is like a friendly chat with your body, a conversation that says, "I've got your back" —pun intended! It's a practical, scientifically-backed technique that empowers you to take control of your stress and anxiety. So, why not take a step toward a more relaxed, focused, and comfortable you? If you're ready to embark on this journey, you're in good company, and the benefits are waiting for you with open arms.

ACTION STEPS

I want you to imagine you're out on a hike surrounded by a lush forest. The path ahead is beautiful, but you keep stumbling over roots because your mind is lost in thought. Your thoughts are like the underbrush that snags your feet, making your journey harder than it needs to be.

Now, let's talk about thought stopping. It's like pulling out a mental compass to navigate this forest. When you notice those overthinking branches tangling you up, stop right there. Take a breath. Picture a stop sign in your mind and say, "Stop!" This simple act interrupts the overthinking cycle.

Have you ever felt overwhelmed by your own thoughts, like they were tripping you up on your life's path?

If you're thinking, "I've tried this before, and it doesn't work," you're not alone. Many of us struggle at first. It's like learning to ride a bike; you might wobble a bit before you find your balance. Consistency is key.

Now, picture this: You're planning a road trip to a place you've never been. You don't have a map or GPS. You could just drive aimlessly and hope to stumble upon your destination, but chances are, you'll get lost or waste time. Overthinking is a lot like that aimless drive, circling around problems without finding solutions.

Here's where problem-solving comes in. It's your trusty map. Think about a problem you're currently facing. Maybe it's work-related or a personal challenge. Write down possible solutions. What are the pros and cons of each? This exercise helps you see the road ahead more clearly.

Have you ever been stuck in a situation where you couldn't see a way out, and your thoughts just kept spinning in circles?

If that sounds familiar, it's time to shift gears. When you break a problem down and analyze it, you're not just a passenger on the overthinking train; you're the engineer, driving toward solutions.

Remember, these techniques might not work overnight. Change takes time and patience. But with practice and perseverance, you can navigate the forest of your thoughts and find clarity. So, the next time you catch yourself overthinking, ask: "Is it time to stop this thought train and start problem-solving instead?" You've got this!

So, my fellow traveler through the maze of the mind, remember this: Overthinking is a habit, and habits can change. You have the power to decide which thoughts you entertain and which ones you let drift away. Isn't that a hopeful thought?

As we wrap up our exploration of strategies for taming overthinking, remember that we can't expect instant results. Just as a garden needs time and care to flourish, so does your mind. In the chapters ahead, we'll explore the art of cultivating a positive

mindset, where you'll discover how to plant the seeds of optimism and nurture them into a vibrant outlook on life. By
combining these strategies with a newfound positivity, you're
on a path toward not just quieting the noise in your mind but
also painting a brighter future. So, let's turn the page and
embark on the journey of growing a more resilient and joyful
mind.

4

CULTIVATING A POSITIVE MINDSET

 The more you overthink the less you will understand.

— HABEEB AKANDE

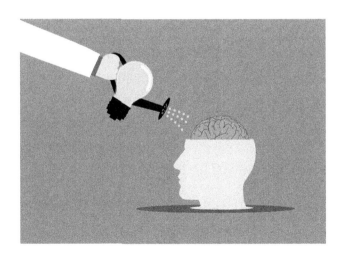

I t is time to explore the incredible impact of developing a positive mindset when it comes to overcoming overthinking. Let me take you on a journey through relatable stories and practical insights that have helped countless individuals break free from the chains of overthinking. Many have been caught in the never-ending loop of analyzing, re-analyzing, and second-guessing every decision, big or small.

Can you envision that you're lying in bed, trying to get a good night's sleep before an important presentation or an exam? But instead of drifting into a peaceful slumber, your mind decides it's the perfect time to replay every awkward moment from the past week and contemplate every possible scenario for tomorrow. Sound familiar? It's a scenario that's played out in countless lives.

Is it really possible to tame this overthinking monster that's been ruling my mind for so long? Well, that's precisely what this chapter aims to address.

Positive thinking is not about putting on rose-colored glasses and pretending that life is perfect. It's about acknowledging the challenges we face while maintaining a hopeful perspective. In fact, research shows that a positive mindset can enhance your resilience, improve problem-solving skills, and even boost your overall well-being (Mayo Clinic, 2022).

But is it really worth the effort to change our thinking patterns? The answer is a resounding yes. And if you're worried about where to start or feeling skeptical about your ability to make this shift, don't worry. We'll walk this path together.

I want you to imagine two friends, Adam and Taylor. They both faced a common challenge in their lives—the relentless cycle of overthinking. Now, let's see how their different mindsets played out in their respective journeys.

Adam had always been a bit of a pessimist. When faced with a problem, the glass was always half-empty. Taylor, on the other hand, had developed a positive mindset over the years. So, what exactly is a positive mindset? It's not about ignoring life's difficulties or living in a world of rainbows and unicorns. It's about choosing to focus on solutions and opportunities rather than dwelling on problems.

One day, both Adam and Taylor faced a challenging situation at work. Their boss assigned them a complex project with a tight deadline. Adam immediately started overthinking. "What if I mess this up? I can't handle the pressure." Thoughts like these overwhelmed Adam, making it difficult to concentrate and taking a toll on his mental well-being.

Taylor approached the same situation with a positive mindset. Instead of dwelling on the potential pitfalls, he asked himself, "What can I learn from this experience? How can I make the most of this opportunity?" Taylor's positive mindset helped him stay focused and creative, ultimately leading to a successful project completion.

Over time, these mindsets had a ripple effect on Adam and Taylor's lives. Adam's constant overthinking not only hindered his work but also spilled over into personal relationships. His friends and family often felt he was distant and always worried about something. Adam's negative mindset became a self-fulfilling prophecy, limiting his growth and happiness.

On the flip side, Taylor's positive mindset transformed his life. It wasn't about ignoring challenges but approaching them with a sense of curiosity and optimism. He found himself more open to new experiences, building stronger connections with others, and, most importantly, experiencing a sense of fulfillment. Instead of dwelling on what might go wrong, Taylor embraced the idea of "What could go right?"

Does this sound a bit too idealistic? Can a simple change in mindset really make that much of a difference? Well, consider this: Research in psychology and neuroscience has shown that a positive mindset can reshape your brain, increasing resilience and reducing the harmful effects of stress (Mayo Clinic, 2022). It's a powerful tool.

A positive mindset takes practice, but did you know that small, consistent steps can lead to lasting change? It's not about being perfect; it's about progress.

If you're thinking to yourself, "I struggle with negativity more often than I'd like," then you're not alone. Many others feel the same way. The good news is that, just like Taylor, you can cultivate a more positive mindset and reap the benefits.

Remember that the power of a positive mindset isn't about denying reality; it's about choosing a different perspective. It's about finding hope and possibility even in the face of challenges. Adam and Taylor's stories show us that with the right mindset, you can reduce overthinking and lead a more fulfilling life. The journey starts with a single thought—what if you could be the Taylor in your own story?

GRATITUDE

I know how it feels to be stuck in life, trust me. In fact, my journey from being stuck to thriving inspired my previous book, *Help Me, I'm Stuck*. Today, I want to talk to you about something that played a crucial role in turning my life around: gratitude.

According to a study, people who practiced gratitude experienced a 15% increase in life satisfaction (Ackerman, 2017). How amazing is that? A simple shift in your mindset can lead to such significant changes in your life.

So, why is gratitude such a benefit? It's all about developing a positive mindset. When we overthink, we often focus on the negatives, magnifying our problems and anxieties. But gratitude flips the script. It forces us to see the positives, no matter how small they may be, and it shifts our perspective toward the good things in life.

Ask yourself, "How can I try to develop gratitude in my daily life?"

Instead of simply writing down what you're grateful for, challenge yourself to find something new and unique each day. It could be a small detail in your surroundings, a fleeting moment, or an unexpected act of kindness you witnessed.

How about taking a mindful walk and focusing solely on things you're grateful for in your environment? Notice the beauty of nature, appreciate the architecture around you, or express gratitude for the opportunity to move and breathe.

If you're artistically inclined, create a gratitude art project. Draw or paint scenes or objects that symbolize what you're thankful for. The act of creating art can deepen your connection to your feelings of gratitude.

Connect with a friend or family member and share your daily gratitude with each other. This not only reinforces your own sense of gratitude but also strengthens your bonds with loved ones.

Try creating a list of things you want to find throughout the day that represent gratitude. It could be finding a heart-shaped stone, a bird's feather, or a person doing a random act of kindness. This keeps you engaged in actively seeking gratitude.

Next, try incorporating gratitude into your daily affirmations. Instead of just affirming your goals, affirm your appreciation for the progress you're making and the lessons you're learning along the way.

Why not create a playlist of songs that evoke feelings of gratitude and joy? Listen to it when you wake up in the morning or during your commute to set a positive tone for your day.

Choose one person each day and perform a random act of kindness to express your gratitude. It could be sending a heartfelt note, sharing a compliment, or cooking their favorite meal.

Challenge yourself to find gratitude in tough situations or setbacks. Ask yourself what you can learn from these experiences and how they might lead to growth or new opportunities.

Why not connect with a friend or family member and share your daily gratitude with each other? This not only reinforces your own sense of gratitude but also strengthens your bonds with loved ones.

Find gratitude in everyday routines and tasks. Express thanks for a warm shower, a good meal, or the ability to read a book. It can remind you of the simple blessings in life.

Instead of listing things you want to achieve in the future, create a "reverse bucket list" of things you've already accomplished or experienced that you're grateful for. It's a powerful reminder of your life's richness.

But let's be real; life isn't all sunshine and rainbows. You might be thinking, "What if I can't find anything to be grateful for on a tough day?" Well, here's where my personal story comes in. I've had days where it felt like the weight of the world was on my shoulders. But even in those moments, I found something small to be grateful for—a ray of sunlight, a kind word from a friend, or the fact that I made it through the day.

So, don't underestimate the power of gratitude. It's a simple yet profound tool that can help you break free from overthinking. Incorporate it into your life, one day at a time, and watch as your mindset shifts toward positivity and hope. You've got this!

SELF-COMPASSION

 Overthinking fades away in the presence of self-love, for in loving oneself, there is no room for doubt or judgment.

— ANONYMOUS

Self-compassion is a powerful concept that involves treating yourself with the same kindness, understanding, and empathy that you would extend to someone you care for or love when you're going through a tough time or facing a mistake or failure. It's about being gentle with yourself, especially in moments of difficulty, and recognizing your own humanity.

How does self-compassion relate to overthinking?

Overthinking often goes hand in hand with self-criticism. When you constantly ruminate on your past actions or worry excessively about the future, it's usually accompanied by a harsh inner dialogue. You might berate yourself for past mistakes or fear future failures. Self-compassion helps to counteract this by encouraging self-kindness instead of self-criticism.

We tend to engage in a lot of negative self-talk when we are overthinking. Self-compassion can actually help you reduce how often you do this. When you approach your thoughts and actions with self-compassion, you're more likely to respond to setbacks with understanding rather than harsh self-criticism. This shift in mindset can decrease the tendency to ruminate and worry excessively.

We overthinkers often set unrealistically high standards for ourselves. We beat ourselves up for not being perfect and dwell on our perceived flaws. Self-compassion encourages you to embrace your imperfections and recognize that nobody is flawless. It's about understanding that making mistakes and experiencing failures is a part of being human, and it doesn't make you any less worthy of kindness and self-acceptance.

A major contributor to stress and anxiety is overthinking. When you're constantly caught up in your thoughts and worrying about everything, it can take a toll on your mental and emotional well-being. Self-compassion has been linked to lower anxiety levels. By soothing your anxious mind with self-compassion, you can find a sense of calm and peace even amidst challenging situations.

Overthinking can become a habit that's hard to break. Self-compassion offers a healthier alternative to this cycle. Instead of ruminating endlessly, you can interrupt the pattern by treating yourself with kindness and giving yourself permission to let go of the overthinking process.

Let's say you are that friend who's running late for that important meeting. The bus you were supposed to catch whizzes by just as you reach the stop. Your inner critic, that nagging voice, starts its usual tirade: "You're so irresponsible! You'll never succeed!" Sound familiar? Most of us have been there at some point.

Now, let's apply a little self-compassion to this situation. Instead of berating yourself, try offering understanding and support. After all, you're human, and humans make mistakes. You might say to yourself, "It happens to the best of us. I can find a way to handle this."

By shifting your inner dialogue from criticism to kindness, you're not just being nice to yourself; you're actually helping yourself perform better under pressure. It's like giving yourself a mental boost, and here's the kicker: scientific research backs this up.

Studies have shown that folks who practice self-compassion tend to have improved mental health. They experience less anxiety and are more resilient in the face of life's ups and downs (Crego et al., 2022). So, if you've ever wondered whether being kind to yourself can actually make a difference, the answer is a resounding yes!

Self-compassion isn't about making excuses or avoiding responsibility. It's about acknowledging your mistakes and shortcomings with empathy rather than self-criticism. In fact, when you treat yourself with kindness, you're more likely to take responsibility for your actions and make positive changes.

Think about it this way: If a friend made a mistake, you wouldn't encourage them to beat themselves up about it. You'd offer support and help them learn from it. So, why not extend the same courtesy to yourself?

Remember, it's a journey. Nobody becomes a self-compassion guru overnight. We all have our moments of self-doubt and self-criticism. Heck, even the person writing this has been there. But the key is to keep practicing and nurturing that self-compassion muscle.

So, I encourage you to be your own best friend. Treat yourself with the kindness and understanding you so readily offer to others. You deserve it, and it can truly transform the way you experience life's challenges. Trust me; you've got this!

I would like to review some practical exercises to get you started on a path of self-compassion:

- **Self-compassionate letter:** Find a quiet space and write a letter to yourself as if you were writing to a friend who's going through a tough time; express understanding, kindness, and support. Acknowledge any pain or suffering you're experiencing. Encourage yourself to be gentle and forgiving toward your own imperfections. Read the letter aloud or keep it handy to remind yourself of your own self-compassion when needed.

- **Personify your inner critic:** Think about that inner voice that's often critical and unkind. Give it a persona or even a name. When you catch yourself being self-critical or overthinking, imagine your inner critic as a separate character. Respond to this inner critic with self-compassion. Kindly and gently challenge its harsh words with more understanding and empathy. For example, the second a negative thought pops into your head, say out loud, "Listen, Lisa, I don't have time for you today, and I am worthy of more than this."
- **Mindful self-compassion:** Practice mindfulness by acknowledging your thoughts and feelings without judgment. When you make a mistake, remind yourself that it's a part of being human.
- **Self-compassion break:** When you face a challenging situation, take a moment to say to yourself, "This is a moment of suffering. Suffering is a part of life. I should be kind to myself."
- **Self-compassion journal:** Start a self-compassion journal where you record moments when you've been self-critical or overthinking. For each instance, write down what triggered it, how it made you feel, and the negative thoughts that arose. Then, practice self-compassion by writing a kind and understanding response to counter those negative thoughts.

Self-compassion is not just another buzzword. It is a scientifically-backed concept (Neff, 2012).

When you treat yourself with kindness, it opens the door to a more positive mindset. You become more motivated to try again after failure, take on new challenges, and nurture your mental well-being. It's like planting seeds of self-encouragement that grow into the tree of resilience.

Remember that self-compassion isn't about ignoring your flaws or becoming complacent. It's about embracing your imperfections and understanding that they make you beautifully human. By cultivating self compassion, you'll not only reduce negative self-talk but also embark on a path toward a happier, more resilient you. So, why not start today? How about giving yourself the goal of showing yourself compassion every day for a week? At the end of the week, ask yourself, "Do I feel better? Is it helping?"

POSITIVE AFFIRMATIONS

You wake up in the morning, and the first thought that crosses your mind is, "Today is going to be a great day!" You smile as you look in the mirror and say to yourself, "I am confident, capable, and ready to tackle whatever comes my way." You carry this positivity with you throughout the day, and it feels like everything just falls into place. Sounds good, right? This is the beauty of positive affirmations.

Positive affirmations are like little notes of encouragement you give to yourself. They're short, powerful statements that help you challenge and overcome self-sabotaging and negative thoughts. They're not about denying reality but rather about

reframing your mindset to create a more positive and productive outlook.

Let's take a real-life scenario. Meet Christine. She used to be
plagued by self-doubt, especially at work. Every time she had to
give a presentation, her mind would flood with thoughts like,
"I'm not good enough," or "I'll mess this up." It was a vicious
cycle, and it was holding her back.

One day, Christine decided to change this. She started by
jotting down her negative thoughts. This was her starting point,
her thought ladder. From there, she rewrote these thoughts into
positive affirmations. Instead of "I'm not good enough," she
wrote, "I am skilled and capable." Whenever self-doubt crept in,
she'd repeat these affirmations to herself, climbing to a new
level of encouragement and empowerment.

Now, think about yourself. What's that one recurring negative
thought you'd like to transform into a positive affirmation?
Take a moment to jot it down. Got it? Great! Now, craft an
affirmation that counters that negative thought. It might feel a
bit strange at first, but trust me, it's worth it.

Positive affirmations aren't just some feel-good exercises. They
can be game-changers in your life. Here are a few benefits to
consider:

- **Reducing overthinking:** I want you to start affirming,
  "I trust my judgment"; you won't believe the peace it
  will bring you. Positive affirmations can silence the
  constant chatter in your mind and help you trust
  yourself more.

- **Promoting positivity:** Do you often find yourself dwelling on negative scenarios or expecting the worst? Affirmations can gently nudge you in the direction of a more optimistic outlook. As you repeat them daily, your brain begins to embrace these positive beliefs.

Scientific studies have shown that positive affirmations can rewire your brain over time (Koosis, 2023). They have a real impact.

So, here's the thing—your mind is incredibly powerful, and it's often your thoughts that can hold you back. But if you're willing to give positive affirmations a try, you're opening the door to a world of potential.

I've been there, struggling with self-doubt and negative thinking. But I've also experienced the transformative power of positive affirmations. They can be your secret weapon to cultivating a positive mindset, reducing overthinking, and bringing more positivity into your life.

Give it a shot, start small, and watch the subtle yet profound changes unfold in your life. I challenge you to try three positive affirmations this week. Be mindful and intentional. After one week, ask yourself if you feel they helped. After all, if you don't try, you'll never know what amazing transformations lie just beyond your doubts. Are you ready to take that step?

AVOIDING NEGATIVE SELF-TALK

Imagine you're driving down a road, and suddenly you hit a pothole. Your car jolts, and you might even hear an unpleasant thud. Now, think of negative self-talk as those mental potholes that can send your thoughts and emotions on a bumpy ride. We all experience them from time to time, but the key is to recognize them and learn how to navigate around them.

Michelle used to have a knack for doubting herself at work. She'd often think, "I'm not smart enough for this job," or "I'll never get that promotion." Michelle felt like she was stuck in a never-ending cycle of self-doubt.

Have you ever found yourself stuck in a similar cycle of self-doubt?

Let's discuss how we recognize these negative thoughts. It's like putting on your detective hat. Start by being mindful of your inner dialogue. When you catch yourself saying things like, "I can't do this," or "I'm not good enough," it's time to raise a mental red flag.

Once you've recognized those negative thoughts, it's time to reframe them. I want you to imagine you're in a beautiful garden, and you notice a few weeds. Instead of dwelling on the weeds, focus on nurturing the beautiful flowers. Similarly, let's weed out those negative thoughts and cultivate positivity.

Techniques for challenging and reframing negative thoughts:

- The "**reality check**" **technique:** If you catch yourself thinking, "I'll never succeed," challenge that thought. Ask yourself, "What evidence do I have to support this?" Often, you'll realize there's little or no basis for your negative belief.

- **The questioning game:** Challenge your negative thoughts by turning them into questions. For example, if you're thinking, "I'm going to mess up this presentation," reframe it as, "Am I really going to mess up this presentation?" Then, objectively explore evidence for and against your negative assumption. This shifts your thinking from a fixed belief to a more open and inquisitive mindset.

- **The probability scale:** Visualize a scale from 0%–100%. When you have a negative thought related to overthinking, ask yourself, "What's the probability that this negative outcome will happen?" Place the thought on the scale according to your estimate. This helps you recognize that most negative scenarios are unlikely to occur and puts things into perspective.

- The "**what if**" **scenario:** Overthinkers often get caught up in "What if?" scenarios that lead to anxiety. Instead of letting these thoughts spiral out of control, use them constructively. Take each "What if" scenario and turn it into an action plan. For example, if you're thinking, "What if I fail the exam?" reframe it as, "What if I study an extra hour each day to improve my chances?"

- **The time-limited analysis:** Allocate a specific amount of time for analyzing a particular issue or negative thought related to overthinking. Once the time is up, make a conscious decision to move on, whether or not you've reached a definitive solution. This prevents rumination and forces you to let go of excessive analysis.

- **The perspective shift:** Imagine you're advising a friend who's facing the same negative thought or overthinking pattern. What advice would you give them? Apply the same compassionate and rational advice to yourself. Sometimes, we're more understanding and objective when helping others, so use this technique to extend that same kindness to yourself.

- **The gratitude and contextualization technique:** When you catch yourself overthinking about a negative event or situation, take a moment to reflect on what you're grateful for in your life. Next, place the negative thought in the broader context of your life and realize that one setback or mistake doesn't define your entire existence.

- **The mindful overthinking:** Instead of trying to stop overthinking altogether, practice mindful overthinking. Set aside a specific time each day to engage in focused overthinking. During this time, allow your mind to explore your concerns, but do so mindfully. Observe your thoughts without judgment, and you may find that over time, your mind naturally begins to settle.

Let's get real here. Negative self-talk can be a real energy drain. When you constantly doubt yourself or dwell on the negative, it's like traveling through water wearing cement shoes. But when you chip away at that cement by reframing your thoughts, something remarkable happens.

Have you ever noticed how your mood shifts when you focus on the positives in your life?

By avoiding negative self-talk, you create space for a more positive mindset. You become your own cheerleader, believing in your abilities, and opening up new possibilities. We're not aiming for an unrealistic outlook. Instead, we're striving for a balanced and realistic perspective. Acknowledging challenges and working through them is essential. In essence, it's about changing the way you talk to yourself. Instead of being your worst critic, become your biggest supporter.

So, here's the takeaway: Negative self-talk is like that pothole on the road of life. By recognizing it, challenging it, and reframing it, you pave the way for a smoother journey toward a more positive and hopeful mindset.

THE ACTION STEPS

Let's begin with gratitude, a powerful force for shifting your perspective. Gratitude practice is like watering the seeds of positivity in your life. Here's how you can start:

- **Gratitude journal:** Get yourself a journal or create a digital one if that suits you better. At the end of each day, jot down three things you are grateful for. Try this for one week and report back to yourself if you feel it was helpful. It could be as simple as a beautiful sunset, a kind word from a friend, or a comforting cup of tea.

- **Morning reflection:** Start your day on a positive note by reflecting on what you're grateful for. Set a goal to spend a few minutes each morning for the next three days, thinking about the blessings in your life. Be sure to check in with yourself to see if you believe this was helpful. Make it a habit to do this before you check your phone or dive into the daily hustle.
- **Share gratitude:** Don't keep your gratitude to yourself. Express it to others. Challenge yourself to send a thank-you note or a heartfelt message to someone who has made a difference in your life just once this week. How did it make you feel? Sharing gratitude multiplies its effects.

Now, let's harness the power of positive affirmations. These are like daily pep talks for your inner self, building a strong foundation of self-belief. Here's how you can create and use them effectively:

- **Identify your goals:** Start by identifying the areas of your life where you'd like to see positive change. It could be confidence, success, or happiness.
- **Craft your affirmations:** Create positive, present-tense statements that align with your goals. For example, "I am confident and capable," "I attract success and abundance," or "I radiate positivity."

- **Repetition is key:** Repeat your affirmations regularly. Say them aloud in front of a mirror, write them down, or set them as daily reminders on your phone. The more you repeat them, the more they become ingrained in your mindset.
- **Believe in them:** As you repeat your affirmations, believe in their truth. Picture yourself embodying these affirmations and visualize the positive outcomes they represent.

Here's an extra step for you. Once you've been diligently practicing gratitude and positive affirmations and you start feeling the positive shifts in your mindset, consider taking a moment to share your experience with others. Your journey can inspire and guide someone else on their path to a positive mindset.

If this book has been a source of inspiration and practical guidance for you, I invite you to share your thoughts by leaving **a review on Amazon**. Your review can serve as a beacon of hope for others seeking transformation. It's a simple action that can have a profound impact on someone's life.

Five-star reviews are the constellation of appreciation in the universe of books.

— ANONYMOUS

These action steps are your tools for cultivating a positive mindset. They may seem small, but remember, even the mightiest trees start as tiny seeds. So, it's time to plant, nurture, and watch your inner garden flourish. Your journey to a brighter and more positive life begins now.

As we wrap up this chapter on fostering a positive mindset, I want you to carry this newfound sense of optimism with you. You've learned the incredible power of gratitude and positive affirmations—tools that can transform your outlook on life. But our journey doesn't end here. In the next chapter, we'll delve into the art of building healthy habits to break free from the clutches of overthinking. Remember, you're not alone on this path, and with each step forward, you're inching closer to a brighter, more fulfilling life. So, let's turn the page and continue our adventure, one positive thought at a time.

5

BUILDING HEALTHY HABITS

It's a good idea to do something relaxing prior to making an important decision in your life.

— PAULO COELHO

This chapter emphasizes the importance of building healthy habits in order to reduce overthinking and improve overall well-being.

Ask yourself, "Can I truly leave behind the chaos of over-thinking and find calm on the other side?" I've been right where you are, caught up in the tumultuous river of my own thoughts, feeling overwhelmed by the currents of anxiety and doubt. It's not easy, and I won't pretend it is. But I'm here to tell you that it is possible. It's a reality within your grasp. Together, we'll explore practical strategies and insights that have helped count-less others make this journey.

THE IMPACT OF HABITS ON OVERTHINKING

You know, overthinking is like that pesky little pebble in your shoe that you can't seem to shake off. It's always there, nagging at you, making every step more uncomfortable than it needs to be. This is not just a minor inconvenience; it's a heavy burden that can weigh you down. When we overthink, we're essentially running on a hamster wheel in our minds, expending precious mental energy without getting anywhere. It leaves us feeling exhausted, stressed, and unable to make clear decisions.

We need to address the importance of daily habits. Imagine your habits as the tools you use to navigate life. If your toolbox is filled with rusty, outdated instruments, it's going to be a lot harder to fix things. Overthinking often stems from negative habits like dwelling on past mistakes, catastrophizing about the future, or comparing ourselves to others. These habits can be deeply ingrained, and it might feel like they're an unchangeable part of who you are. But guess what? We can replace those rusty tools with shiny new ones. Research has shown that establishing positive habits can rewire your brain over time (McLachlan, 2021). It's like renovating a house—it takes some effort, but the end result is a beautiful, more functional space. So, let's start building those positive habits, one step at a time, and give overthinking a run for its money! Let's roll up our sleeves and get to work on that mental renovation project.

How can you replace those pesky negative habits of over-thinking with some positive ones? Imagine it like decluttering your mental space, making room for more peace and clarity.

- **Identify the culprits:** Let's identify those negative habits that are feeding the overthinking monster. It could be replaying conversations in your head, constantly checking your email, or dwelling on what went wrong in the past. Pinpoint these habits and write them down. Awareness is the first step to change.

- **Start small:** Begin with small, manageable changes. For example, if you find yourself ruminating about the past, commit to setting aside just five minutes a day for this, and then gradually decrease it over time. It's like weaning yourself off a bad habit.

- **Replace, don't erase:** Trying to eliminate a habit altogether can be tough. Instead, focus on replacing it with something positive. If you're always checking your phone, replace that with a quick walk outside or a chat with a friend. It's about redirecting your energy in a healthier way.

- **Set clear goals:** Make your intentions crystal clear. Instead of saying, "I want to stop overthinking," say, "I will spend 10 minutes journaling my thoughts before bedtime to clear my mind." Specific goals are easier to measure and attain.

- **Track your progress:** Keep a journal or use a habit-tracking app to monitor your progress. This not only holds you accountable but also provides a sense of accomplishment as you see your positive habits replacing the negative ones. Give yourself a goal of 15 minutes a day to practice journaling.

- **Accountability partner:** Share your goals with a friend or loved one who can help keep you on track.

Sometimes, having someone to encourage you makes all the difference. Make an agreement with a friend to share a 20-minute conversation once a week.

- **Mindfulness and self-compassion:** Practice mindfulness to stay in the present moment and be aware of when you're slipping into old habits of overthinking. Try aiming for 15 minutes of mindfulness and self-compassion when you first wake up and just before going to sleep. And remember, it's okay to stumble along the way. Be kind to yourself and acknowledge that change takes time.

Are you wondering if you will be able to maintain these new habits? It's entirely normal to slip up from time to time. The key is not to beat yourself up over it. It's a journey, and everyone takes a few detours. The important thing is to get back on track and keep moving forward.

EXERCISE AND PHYSICAL ACTIVITY

 Exercise is the off-switch for the overthinking mind, where worries evaporate, and clarity finds its path.

— ANONYMOUS

I would like to look at how exercise can be your secret weapon against overthinking and boost your mental health. I promise this isn't some far-fetched idea; it's grounded in science and simple, actionable steps that anyone can take. So, let's get real and practical!

Those sleepless nights when your mind is racing a hundred miles an hour with thoughts and worries? Yep, I've had my fair share of those. But did you know that exercise can be your ally in taming that overactive mind?

It's all about brain chemistry. When you exercise, your body releases endorphins, those feel-good chemicals. They act as natural mood lifters, helping to reduce anxiety and stress.

Here are some practical tips to make exercise a part of your daily life and stop that overthinking:

- **Set micro-goals:** Instead of focusing on big fitness goals, set micro-goals that are easy to achieve. For example, commit to doing just five minutes of exercise each day. It's a small, manageable step that can help you overcome the mental hurdle of starting.

- **The "two-minute rule"**: Tell yourself that you'll engage in exercise for just two minutes. Once you start, you might find it easier to continue. This tactic is particularly effective for breaking the overthinking loop.

- **Combine exercise with mindfulness:** Practice mindfulness during your workout. Pay attention to the physical sensations, your breath, and the environment around you. This can help divert your mind from overthinking and make exercise more enjoyable.

- **Variety is key:** Avoid getting stuck in a monotonous exercise routine. Try different activities, whether it's hiking, dancing, or martial arts. Variety can keep exercise exciting and reduce overthinking about the same repetitive routine.

- **Social exercise:** Join a group fitness class or find a workout buddy. Socializing while exercising can make it more enjoyable and help you get out of your head, reducing overthinking.

- **Create a fun playlist:** Music can be a powerful motivator. Create a workout playlist filled with your favorite energetic tunes. It can distract you from overthinking and make exercise more enjoyable.

- **Incorporate playfulness:** Think back to activities you enjoyed as a child, such as jumping on a trampoline or playing tag. Incorporate playful elements into your exercise routine to make it feel less like a chore.

- **Mindful walking or running:** If you enjoy walking or running, turn it into a mindfulness exercise. Pay attention to your surroundings, the sensation of your feet hitting the ground, and your breathing. This can help you stay present and reduce overthinking.
- **Visualization and affirmations:** Before your workout, visualize yourself enjoying the exercise and feeling energized. Use positive affirmations like, "I am strong and capable," to boost your confidence and reduce overthinking.
- **Reward yourself creatively:** Set up a rewards system for yourself. However, make it unique and interesting. For example, treat yourself to a special tea, a relaxing bath, or an episode of your favorite TV show after each workout.
- **Exercise as problem-solving time:** Use your exercise sessions as dedicated problem-solving or brainstorming time. Often, physical activity can stimulate creativity and help you find solutions to the issues you're overthinking.
- **Track progress creatively:** Instead of traditional tracking methods, like numbers on a scale, use creative ways to track your progress. Create a visual art project or a journal to document your fitness journey.

Even 20 minutes a day can make a significant difference. Think of it as an investment in your mental well-being.

And if you're worried about the gym atmosphere or feeling self-conscious, don't be. You can exercise at home, in a park, or anywhere that makes you comfortable.

Numerous studies have shown the mental health benefits of exercise. For instance, a study published found that exercise can reduce symptoms of depression and anxiety (Craft & Perna, 2004).

So, lace up those sneakers and let's get moving toward a brighter, more balanced mind!

SLEEP AND REST

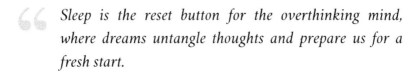

> *Sleep is the reset button for the overthinking mind, where dreams untangle thoughts and prepare us for a fresh start.*

— ANONYMOUS

We're all guilty of overthinking from time to time, and I'm right there with you on this journey to calm our racing minds.

Why is sleep so important for curbing overthinking and boosting our mental well-being? Well, science has got our back on this one. Research shows that inadequate sleep messes with our brain's ability to function properly (Suni, 2016). It's like trying to run a marathon with your shoes tied together!

When we don't get enough quality shut-eye, our brain's emotional center goes into overdrive, making us more susceptible to stress and anxiety. But there is good news: By prioritizing sleep and rest, we can tame that overthinking beast. Let's explore some practical tips to establish a healthier sleep routine:

- **Consistent bedtime:** Pick a bedtime and stick to it, even on weekends. This helps regulate your body's internal clock, making it easier to fall asleep and wake up feeling refreshed.
- **Create a relaxing bedtime routine:** Wind down before bed by reading, taking a warm bath, or doing some gentle stretches. This signals to your body that it's time to relax.
- **Optimize your sleep environment:** Make your sleep space comfortable and conducive to rest. A comfy mattress, cozy blankets, and a dark, cool room are your best friends.
- **Limit screen time:** Blue light from screens messes with your sleep hormones. Try to avoid screens at least an hour before bedtime. You can do it!

- **Watch what you eat and drink:** Avoid heavy meals, caffeine, and alcohol close to bedtime. These can disrupt your sleep.
- **Limit naps:** While short power naps can be great, try not to nap for too long during the day, as it can interfere with nighttime sleep.
- **Be patient:** Be patient with yourself. If you can't fall asleep or wake up in the middle of the night, don't stress about it. Stress only makes it worse.

Remember, we're not aiming for perfection here. Slip-ups happen, and that's okay. The key is to create a routine that works for you and makes sleep a priority.

I know what you might be thinking: "I'm too busy for this!" But remember, prioritizing sleep and rest is an investment in your mental health and overall well-being. You'll find that with better sleep, your overthinking tendencies will start to calm down, and you'll have a clearer, more focused mind during the day.

So, go ahead and give these tips a try. It might take some time, but with a little patience and persistence, you'll find that peaceful sleep and a quieter mind are well within your reach. Sweet dreams and a brighter, less overthinking-filled tomorrow await!

NUTRITION AND DIET

 Good nutrition is the fuel that powers the mind, turning the chaos of overthinking into a well-oiled machine of clarity.

— ANONYMOUS

I know it might sound like a bit of a leap, but trust me, what you put on your plate can have a significant influence on how you think and feel.

I can relate to those nights when you can't stop replaying that awkward conversation in your head or stressing over tomorrow's big meeting. Overthinking can be a real struggle, and it's something I've grappled with myself. By making some practical changes to your diet, you can ease that mental turmoil.

I'm not going to hit you with a bunch of complicated nutritional jargon. We're keeping this down-to-earth and approachable. So, here's the deal: Our brains need a balanced diet to function at their best. You see, your brain is like a finely-tuned machine, and the fuel it runs on is the food you eat.

Start by making sure you're getting a balance of nutrients in each meal. That means incorporating protein, complex carbohydrates, and healthy fats. Protein helps with the production of neurotransmitters like serotonin and dopamine, which can influence your mood and thoughts. Complex carbs provide a steady source of energy, and healthy fats are essential for brain health.

Omega-3 fatty acids are a must. These little wonders are found in fatty fish like salmon, flaxseeds, and walnuts. Omega-3s have been linked to improved cognitive function and mood stabilization. So, consider adding more of these to your diet.

Veggies like spinach, kale, and broccoli are packed with antioxidants that help protect your brain cells from oxidative stress. They're also rich in vitamins and minerals that support mental well-being.

Don't forget the importance of staying hydrated! Even mild dehydration can affect your mood and cognitive function. Sip on water throughout the day to keep your brain in tip-top shape.

Here's the part you might not like to hear. Excessive sugar and processed foods can wreak havoc on your mood and mental clarity. They lead to energy spikes and crashes, making it harder to keep those thoughts in check. Try to reduce your intake of these culprits.

Okay, I hear you thinking, "But what about my favorite comfort foods?" Don't worry; you don't have to give them up entirely. It's all about balance. Treat yourself occasionally, but make sure the foundation of your diet is built on those brain-boosting nutrients.

Remember, it's not a one-size-fits-all solution. Your body is unique, and what works for someone else might not work for you. So, be patient and give your dietary changes some time to show their effects on your mental well-being.

MINDFUL TECHNOLOGY USE

It's time to dive straight into the world of technology, that double-edged sword we can't seem to live without. It's an incredible tool that has made our lives more convenient in countless ways. But it can also be a major contributor to over-thinking. So, here's the lowdown on mindful technology use and how to develop healthier habits around it.

You know that feeling when you're scrolling through your social media feed late at night, and suddenly you stumble upon a post that triggers a whirlwind of thoughts and self-compar-isons? Or when you're bombarded with notifications from work emails, messages from friends, and news updates? Yep, that's how technology often adds fuel to the overthinking fire.

Research has shown that constant exposure to screens and notifications can increase stress levels and negatively impact our mental well-being (Amistad, 2023). Our brains are wired to react to novel information, and the digital world provides an endless stream of it. No wonder our thoughts can spiral out of control!

We need to have a look at practical steps to regain control of your tech use and stop overthinking:

- **Set boundaries:** You need to set clear boundaries for when and how you use your devices. Designate tech-free times during the day, especially before bedtime. Your bedroom should be a sanctuary, not an extension of your office.
- **Mindful notifications:** Take charge of your notifications. Turn off nonessential ones. Limit the apps that can send you alerts. By doing this, you're choosing what you engage with, rather than being reactive to every ping.
- **Digital detox:** Consider regular digital detox periods. Try a day or weekend without screens. Use this time for activities that truly relax and rejuvenate you, like reading a book, going for a walk, or practicing a hobby.
- **Mindful scrolling:** When you're on social media, be conscious of your intention. Are you mindlessly scrolling to kill time, or are you genuinely connecting with friends and enjoying content that adds value to

your life? Unfollow accounts that don't serve your well-being.

- **Embrace real-life connections:** Make an effort to connect with people in the physical world. Invite a friend for coffee or take your spouse for a walk in the park. Real human interactions can be a wonderful antidote to overthinking.

It's okay to struggle with these changes. We all do. But with small, consistent steps, you can gradually shift your relationship with technology. Start by picking one of these tips that resonates with you and give it a shot.

THE ACTION STEPS

- **Create a routine:** Think of your daily routine as your trusty anchor, holding you steady in the turbulent sea of thoughts. Take a moment to ponder: What activities or habits can you incorporate into your morning routine to set a positive tone for the day? It might be as simple as sipping on your favorite tea, doing a quick stretch, or jotting down a gratitude list. The goal here is to start your day with intention and positivity. Calendars, written or digital, are a great addition here. They can help you stay on track.
- **Exercise:** Exercise is like a kickstart for your brain, pumping out endorphins and tossing stress to the curb. But it doesn't have to be a grueling gym session–it can be something as enjoyable as a brisk walk, dancing to

your favorite music, or a refreshing swim. Ask yourself: "What types of exercise do I enjoy?" How can you incorporate more exercise into your daily routine? Maybe a 15-minute morning stretch or a short evening stroll? Whatever gets you moving and feeling good.

Life can get pretty hectic, and it's easy to make excuses to avoid these things. But here's the thing—these small changes can make a big difference.

Let's be real here: Nobody's got it all figured out, including me. We all have our moments of self-doubt and overthinking. But we can make progress. It's about taking one step at a time and being kind to ourselves along the way.

6

STAYING PRESENT AND FOCUSED

You only have control over three things in your life, the thoughts you think, the images you visualize, and the actions you take.

— JACK CANFIELD

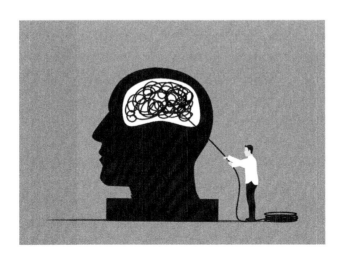

I t's a beautiful sunny day, and you're sitting on a park bench, enjoying the warmth of the sun on your skin. Your surroundings are serene, with birds chirping, leaves rustling in the gentle breeze, and the distant laughter of children playing. It's a perfect moment, right? Although you notice your mind is racing a million miles an hour, lost in a whirlwind of worries, regrets, and hypothetical situations. You're physically present, but your thoughts have wandered far from this tranquil setting.

We've all been there, struggling to be fully present in the moment. And that's precisely what this chapter is all about— bringing you back to the here and now, where you can find peace, clarity, and the power to conquer overthinking.

I want you to know I can relate, I've been right where you are, battling the same mental chaos. I know how overwhelming it can be when your thoughts are on overdrive, making it nearly impossible to appreciate the beauty of a sunny day, a warm cup of tea, or even the company of a loved one.

I'm here to share practical advice. Instead, we'll explore simple yet effective methods to tame the overthinking beast. And when those doubts creep in, as they inevitably will, I'll be here to address your objections and keep you on track.

THE BENEFITS OF STAYING PRESENT AND FOCUSED

Studies have shown that our brains are wired to overthink. It's a survival mechanism started by our ancestors long before we were born (Jay, 2020). Back in the day, being hypervigilant about potential threats meant staying alive. But in today's world, it often leads to unnecessary stress and anxiety.

Here's where staying present and focused comes in. When you're fully engaged in the here and now, your brain doesn't have the time or energy to wander into the treacherous terrain of overthinking. You're not ruminating about the past or worrying about the future; you're right where you need to be.

Reducing overthinking can lead to so many wonderful benefits. When you're not constantly mulling over past mistakes or fretting about what might happen tomorrow, your stress levels drop. It's like taking a load off your shoulders.

Ever made a snap judgment because your mind was racing? Staying present helps you make more thoughtful, informed decisions. It's like having your own personal decision-making coach.

When you're fully focused on the task at hand, you're bound to get more done. No more wasted time on unnecessary mental detours. As well, remaining present in your interactions with others means you're really listening, empathizing, and connecting. Your husband, wife, or even friend will appreciate it.

Living in the moment tends to make you happier. You'll savor life's little joys and find contentment in the simplest things. If you're thinking *"That all sounds great, but how on earth do I actually stay present and focused?"* Excellent question! Let's get practical:

The Pomodoro Technique:

- **How it works:** This time-management method breaks tasks into short, focused intervals—usually 25 minutes—called "pomodoros," followed by a 5-minute break. Every fourth break is longer, around 15 minutes. This pattern helps maintain high levels of focus and gives your brain "mini rests" to recharge. It prevents burnout, overthinking, and maintains a high level of productivity throughout a task.

Tech-free time:

- **How it works:** Allocate specific periods during the day when you put away all electronic devices. This means no phones, tablets, or laptops. Instead, engage in offline activities like reading a physical book, cooking, or taking a walk. This reduces distractions and allows your mind to focus on one task or enjoy a genuine rest.

Task batching:

- **How it works:** Group similar tasks together and tackle them in one go. For instance, if you have several emails to send or meetings to set up, do them all in one designated time block rather than sporadically throughout the day. It reduces the mental load of constantly switching between tasks, making you more efficient and present in each activity.

Physical anchors:

- **How it works:** Use physical sensations or actions to bring you back to the present. This could be as simple as snapping a rubber band on your wrist, gripping your chair, or feeling the texture of your desk under your fingertips. Physical sensations can act as an instant reminder to be present, pulling your attention back to the here and now.

Start small, be patient with yourself, and keep reminding yourself of the fantastic benefits that come with staying present and focused. Your journey to a calmer, more focused you begins today.

UNDERSTANDING MIND WANDERING

Mind wandering is something we've all experienced. It's that moment when you're supposed to be focusing on a task at hand —let's say, listening to your spouse discuss weekend plans—but your mind drifts off to a distant memory or an imaginary scenario. Suddenly, you're thinking about that thing you said three years ago, or what you'll cook for dinner next week. Oops!

Mind wandering is like your mind's little vacation. It's when your thoughts disconnect from the present and float away. While this can sometimes be a pleasant escape—daydreaming about a beach while sitting in a meeting? Guilty as charged—it can also lead to overthinking, especially if our mind wanders to worries, past regrets, or future anxieties.

Research has shown that mind wandering can be both a gift and a curse. A study published found that people's minds wandered about 47% of the time, irrespective of what they were doing (Escalante, 2021). That's almost half our waking hours!

This same study found that people were generally less happy when their minds were wandering. The act of drifting away from the present, especially to negative or uncertain scenarios, can lead to feelings of unhappiness or dissatisfaction. Over time, this can become a habit, and before you know it, you're stuck in a cycle of overthinking (Escalante, 2021).

When our minds constantly drift to "problem scenarios," we start creating issues that may not even exist. It's like a snowball effect. One small, seemingly harmless thought rolls and grows until it becomes an overwhelming avalanche.

You might object, "But isn't it good to prepare for the worst? To anticipate problems?" Sure, a bit of foresight is excellent. But there's a fine line between productive planning and endless rumination. Overthinking often paralyzes us, making us more hesitant and less decisive.

Below, you will find seven practical suggestions to navigate mind wandering:

1. **A mental "SWAT" team:** Visualize a mini SWAT team inside your head, ready to intervene when your mind wanders. Every time you catch yourself drifting,

imagine them swooping in, getting your thoughts in order, and guiding them back to the task at hand.

2. **Thought-taming alarm:** Set random alarms throughout the day. When it goes off, it acts as a cue for you to check in on your thoughts. Are you daydreaming or focused? This increases your awareness of your mental state.

3. **The "not now" box:** Have a small box or container at your desk or workspace. Whenever a distracting thought enters your mind, write it down on a piece of paper and put it in the box. This symbolic act allows you to acknowledge the thought but defer it for later.

4. **Environment switch:** If you find your mind frequently wandering in a particular setting, change it up. Move to a different room, work from a coffee shop, or simply rearrange your workspace. A fresh environment often stimulates focus.

5. **The mind's soundtrack:** Create a playlist of instrumental songs or ambient sounds. This isn't just background noise. Every time your mind wanders, focus on a single instrument or sound. It's a gentle nudge to return to your current task.

6. **Active doodling:** Keep a doodle pad beside you. When your mind starts to wander, start doodling but with a twist. Your doodles should be related to the topic you're working on or the task at hand, turning distractions into productive visual notes. For example, if you are working on a work presentation for an ad on coffee, doodle cute, animated coffee cups!

7. **The mindful sip:** Always have a beverage nearby, be it water, tea, or coffee. When your mind strays, take a deliberate sip. Feel the temperature, taste, and sensation as you swallow. It's a simple way to center yourself.

So, let's stop being trapped by our wandering minds. Let's be present, live in the moment, and enjoy the journey of life. After all, a wandering mind is an unhappy mind, but a mind in the present is focused.

THE ACTION STEPS

Isn't it amazing how our brains, with their millions of neurons firing away, have the capability to juggle a million thoughts at once? I mean, sure, it's impressive. But let's be real, it's also exhausting. I've found myself tumbling down the rabbit hole of overthinking more times than I'd like to admit. But I've also learned ways to snap out of it. I've combed through scientific studies and tried-and-tested techniques to curate the best action steps for you. So, whether you're ruminating about that conversation with your spouse from two weeks ago or stressing about that looming work deadline, I've got your back.

- **Mindful breathing:** Hear me out. Breathing might seem like such a basic, "everyone-does-it" function, but how many of us truly breathe mindfully?

○ **The 4-7-8 breathing technique:**

1. Inhale for a count of four.
2. Hold that breath for a count of seven.
3. Exhale slowly over a count of eight.

This isn't just about counting. It's about grounding yourself in the present. So, the next time you find your thoughts spiraling, pause and take a few of these breaths. I personally swear by it on those particularly challenging days.

- **Single-tasking:** You've probably heard about multi-tasking and how it's the future. Well, here's a fun twist: It's not. Single-tasking is where it's at. The act of dedicating yourself entirely to one task not only improves the quality of your work but also allows you to complete it faster.
- **Choose one task:** Be it washing the dishes, writing a report, or talking with your spouse. For the next hour, rid yourself of all distractions, phones, tablets, the TV, put them away. Now, dive deep into your chosen task, giving it your undivided attention.
- **The "why" journal:** This is a little trick I've picked up: Whenever I catch myself overthinking, I write down my thoughts and ask myself, "Why?" Why am I feeling this way? Why is this bothering me so much? This doesn't mean you need a full-blown journaling session, but by putting the thought on paper, you're literally taking it out of your head. It not only helps you

understand your feelings better, but it also calms the brain!

- **Physical grounding techniques:** When your mind races, ground your body. Simple activities like stamping your feet, clapping your hands, or even holding onto an object and focusing on its texture can divert your attention from those swirling thoughts. The idea here is to connect with the tangible, the real, the now.

And there we are, having journeyed through the intricate labyrinth of our minds, standing at the precipice of understanding and transformation. The power of the present moment is both a gift and a challenge. Overthinking, as we've unraveled, has a crafty way of robbing us of this gift, stealing away those golden moments when we could be truly alive and engaged.

Yet, in these pages, we've armed ourselves with the tools and insights to reclaim that stolen time. With each strategy we've embraced, we've taken a stand against the torrent of endless thoughts, affirming that while our minds are vast and wandering, we have the power to guide them.

The journey thus far hasn't been about silencing our thoughts—that would be denying the essence of our beautifully complex minds. Instead, it's been about mastering them, understanding their rhythms, and ensuring they dance to the music we play, not the other way around.

As we turn the page to our final chapter, let's carry forward this momentum. You've come so far, embraced change, and navigated challenges. Ahead lies the essential task of maintaining this progress, ensuring the shifts you've experienced become the bedrock of your daily life.

Hold your head high; the next steps are about cementing this newfound presence and focus it into every facet of your life. The best part? You're already equipped, empowered, and on your way.

7

MAINTAINING PROGRESS

> *We can not solve our problems with the same level of thinking that created them.*

— ALBERT EINSTEIN

As we embark on this final chapter of our journey together, I want to acknowledge the incredible progress you've made. You've demonstrated a deep commitment to making meaningful changes in your life, and I commend you for it.

Our journey has been about more than just understanding why overthinking plagues us; it's been about equipping ourselves with a powerful set of tools and strategies to navigate through it. Think of this chapter as understanding that new toolbox, ready to assist whenever you find yourself spiraling down the overthinking rabbit hole. These tools are tried-and-tested strategies backed by science and experience.

We all will wonder how we can ensure we continue to make progress, and what if we stumble along the way? These concerns are entirely valid, and this chapter is designed to address them head-on.

In the upcoming pages, we will explore three potent approaches: self-reflection, accountability, and self-care practices.

It may seem overwhelming at first. You might be thinking, "How can I possibly incorporate all of this into my daily routine?" or "I've tried some of these strategies before, and they didn't work for me." To that, I say that every individual is unique, and what didn't work in the past might simply require a slight adjustment to succeed. Remember, consistency is the key. It's not about making giant leaps but rather taking small, consistent steps that lead to lasting change.

So, are you prepared to dive in, free from the burden of over-thinking about diving in? Let's begin this final leg of our journey. Armed with knowledge and a great toolbox, we are poised to bid farewell to overthinking and welcome a more fulfilling, empowering, and meaningful life.

SELF-REFLECTION

 Self reflection is the mirror that reveals the roots of overthinking, and in its gentle gaze, we find the path to inner calm.

— ANONYMOUS

Self-reflection is like a mirror for your thoughts and feelings. It's your way of hitting pause in the midst of your mental chaos and taking a good, hard look at what's going on inside. It's not about blaming yourself or dwelling on past mistakes; it's about understanding your thought patterns and emotions.

So, why should you bother with self-reflection when you just want to stop overthinking? Self-reflection is a huge component to breaking free from the chains of overthinking.

Self-reflection helps you become aware of your overthinking habits. It's like shining a light on the dark corners of your mind. When you know what triggers your overthinking, you can start addressing it.

By reflecting on your thoughts and emotions, you can gain valuable insights into why you overthink. Maybe it's fear of the unknown, a need for control, or a deep-seated belief in perfection. Knowing the "why" is a big part of the solution.

Let's say you're in a meeting, and you keep replaying a moment where you stumbled over your words. Self-reflection might reveal that your overthinking in this situation stems from a fear of judgment. Armed with this insight, you can work on building confidence or adopting techniques to manage that fear.

Techniques for Self-Reflection

Now that we understand why self-reflection is a game-changer, let's explore some practical techniques to get you started:

- **The "Mind Map" method:** Grab a blank sheet of paper and place a central idea or thought in the middle. Now, let your mind wander and jot down any related thoughts or emotions as branches and sub-branches.

This visual representation can help you see how your thoughts are connected and identify patterns.

- **The "Photo Diary" approach:** Take a photo of something that captures your emotions or thoughts at various points during your day. It could be a sunset, your desk cluttered with work, or a cup of coffee. Later, review these photos and write a few sentences about what each one represents for you. This creative approach can reveal a lot about your inner world.

- **The "Character Dialogue" exercise:** Imagine you're a character in a book or a movie. Write a conversation between yourself and this character. Ask them questions about your thoughts, feelings, and actions. It's like having an honest heart-to-heart with your fictional twin.

- **The "Letter to Your Past Self" technique:** Write a letter to a younger version of yourself. Reflect on the advice and comfort you'd offer. This exercise can help you understand how you've grown and what lessons you've learned from your past experiences.

- **The "Emotion Timeline" visualization:** Close your eyes and visualize your life as a timeline. Place various emotions on this timeline to represent when you've felt them most strongly. This can help you identify patterns in your emotional journey and pinpoint moments that triggered overthinking.

- **The "Empty Room" visualization:** Picture an empty room. Now, fill it with objects or symbols that represent your thoughts, worries, and emotions. Imagine organizing or removing these items as a way of decluttering your mind. It's a creative way to mentally tidy up.

- **The "Voice Journal" technique:** Instead of writing, record your thoughts and reflections in an audio journal. Hearing your own voice can bring a different dimension to self-reflection and make it feel like you're having a conversation with yourself.
- **The "Nondominant Hand Writing" exercise:** If you're right-handed, try writing with your left hand—and vice versa. This disrupts your usual thought patterns and can reveal deeper, less-filtered insights because your dominant hand is less involved in the process.
- **The "Favorite Quote" reflection:** Choose a favorite quote or saying that resonates with you. Reflect on why it resonates and how it applies to your life. This can serve as a thought-provoking starting point for self-reflection.
- **The "Silent Mindfulness" practice:** Find a quiet space, close your eyes, and simply focus on your breath for a few minutes. Instead of actively thinking, try to observe your thoughts as they come and go without judgment. It's a way to create mental space for self-reflection.

These techniques cater to various learning styles and preferences, so you can pick the one that resonates with you the most. Remember, self-reflection is a personal journey, and it's all about understanding yourself better. So, embrace these creative approaches and use them as tools to uncover your inner thoughts and emotions. Happy reflecting!

ACCOUNTABILITY

Imagine you're setting out on a road trip to a beautiful destination. You've got your map—your plan to stop overthinking—and your car—your willpower. But there's one thing missing—a co-pilot, otherwise known as your accountability partner who keeps you on track and ensures you reach your destination.

Accountability partners can provide that much-needed motivation when your enthusiasm wanes. They remind you why you started this journey in the first place. It's like having a built-in GPS for your goals. They will help you stay on course, follow a structured plan, and reach your destination faster. Sometimes, you're too close to a problem to see the solution. Accountability partners can offer fresh perspectives and constructive feedback.

So, how does one find this accountability partner? There are plenty of online communities and groups dedicated to personal growth and self-improvement. Join one related to your goal and start engaging. I have listed some below (Mitchell, 2023):

- **MensGroup:** This website is committed to creating a virtual community where men can come together, fostering connections, and offering support in their personal growth journeys. It provides a secure and accepting environment where men can openly discuss their experiences, challenges, and insights on various subjects, including relationships, careers, and mental well-being.
- **Deciding To Be Better:** This is a subreddit dedicated to providing a space where people interested in personal

growth and self-improvement can come together. As their community ethos declares, "We believe in progress, so if you've made the choice to move away from the negative, you're in the right place." Within this subreddit, you'll discover a nurturing atmosphere where you can openly discuss your personal experiences, challenges, and insights on various subjects, including mental well-being, productivity, empowerment, and relationships.

- **GetMotivated**: This subreddit garners a substantial following of individuals in search of inspiration and motivation. It serves as a forum where people from diverse backgrounds can unite and exchange motivational quotes, anecdotes, and images with the aim of motivating and uplifting one another.

To find an accountability partner, you can also recruit a friend, colleague, or family member who shares your goal. The beauty here is the mutual motivation you can provide each other. Or, if you're looking for professional guidance, consider hiring a coach. They're trained to keep you accountable, and their expertise can be exactly what you need.

TOOLS TO TRACK PROGRESS

Let's discuss ways to track your progress. This isn't about dredging through endless spreadsheets; it's about finding tools that work for you:

- **Visual progress board:** Create a visual board or collage that represents your journey to overcome overthinking. Use images, quotes, and symbols that resonate with your goals. Update it regularly to visually track your progress and remind yourself of your objectives.
- **Progress timeline:** Create a timeline or chart where you can map out your progress over weeks or months. Note significant milestones, insights gained, and challenges overcome. This provides a visual representation of your growth.
- **Habit tracking apps:** Utilize habit-tracking apps like HabitBull or Streaks to monitor your efforts in implementing the tips found throughout this book. You can set specific goals related to reducing overthinking and mark each day you successfully follow the recommended strategies.
- **Emotion tracking apps:** Some apps, like Moodnotes or Daylio, allow you to track your emotions throughout the day. This can help you correlate emotional states with overthinking episodes and assess how well you're managing your emotions over time.
- **AI-based mood analyzers:** There are AI-driven apps and tools that can analyze your written or spoken words to detect emotional patterns. These can provide insights into your emotional state and help you track improvements in managing overthinking.
- **Data visualization software:** If you're technically inclined, you can use data visualization software like Tableau or Excel to create interactive graphs and charts

tracking your overthinking episodes and progress. This can make your journey more engaging and insightful.

Embrace the power of accountability in your quest to stop overthinking. Use these strategies, find the right partner, and choose tools that resonate with you. Your journey might have its twists and turns, but with accountability, you'll find your way to a more peaceful, less overburdened mind.

SELF-CARE PRACTICES

Self-care is the soothing balm for an overthinking mind, a reminder that we are worthy of the same kindness we freely give to others.

— ANONYMOUS

What is self-care, you ask? Well, it's not just about bubble baths and scented candles, although those can be delightful. Self-care is all about taking deliberate actions to maintain and improve your overall well-being. Think of it as nurturing your mind, body, and soul, much like you'd care for a beloved plant or pet. It's a way to recharge your batteries and show yourself the love and attention you truly deserve.

So, how can self-care help you kick the habit of overthinking? Let's break it down.

Research has shown that regular self-care can significantly reduce stress levels (Kapil, 2022). When you're less stressed, your mind is less likely to spiral into overthinking mode. Try incorporating stress-reducing activities like deep breathing exercises or even a short daily walk into your routine.

Self-care encourages mindfulness, which, as we've discussed, is all about being present in the moment. When you're fully engaged in what you're doing, there's less room for those nagging, repetitive thoughts.

Taking care of your emotional health is vital. Engage in activities that bring you joy and satisfaction, whether it's painting, dancing, or playing an instrument. These activities release feel-good hormones that can help combat overthinking.

And let's not forget about our physical health. A healthy body supports a healthy mind. Prioritize regular exercise and nourishing your body with nutritious foods. Exercise releases endorphins, which are natural mood lifters. A healthier you is less likely to overthink.

Spending quality time with loved ones is a powerful form of self-care. Strong social connections can provide a support system to help you manage overthinking. Share your feelings with a trusted friend or family member—it's okay not to go through everything alone.

Let's explore some unique tips for integrating self-care into your daily life:

- **Set self-care appointments:** Just like you schedule meetings and work tasks, schedule self-care activities. Treat them with the same level of importance. Block out time in your calendar for self-care, whether it's a 20-minute break for a mindful walk or a longer slot for a hobby you enjoy.
- **The power of micro self-care:** If you're crunched for time, don't worry; even small acts of self-care count. Take a moment to savor your morning coffee, do some quick stretching exercises, or practice deep breathing during your commute. Every little bit helps.
- **Self-care kit:** Create a self-care toolkit filled with things that bring you comfort and joy—your favorite book, a cozy blanket, soothing tea, or calming music. Having these at hand can help you unwind whenever you need it.
- **Self-compassion:** Be kind to yourself. Remember that nobody is perfect, and we all have our struggles, including me. Don't beat yourself up if you catch yourself overthinking. Instead, acknowledge it and gently guide your mind back to the present moment.

Remember, it's all about progress, not perfection. So, don't be discouraged if you hit a few bumps along the way. Stay hopeful and keep experimenting with different self-care practices until you discover the ones that truly resonate with you.

Now, get out there and start embracing self-care as your ally in the battle against overthinking.

HANDLING SETBACKS

I would like to start by addressing the common setbacks that you might encounter on your journey to curb overthinking. These are the stumbling blocks that can make you feel like you're taking two steps forward and one step back.

Many of us experience negative self-talk. It's that nagging voice in your head that says, "You're not good enough" or "You'll never succeed." Negative self-talk can be a significant setback because it fuels overthinking. When you catch yourself in this loop, remember that it's just your mind playing tricks on you. Challenge those negative thoughts with evidence to the contrary.

Cognitive distortions are thinking patterns that twist reality, making situations seem worse than they are. Examples include catastrophizing—imagining the worst-case scenario—and black-and-white thinking. To combat cognitive distortions, practice recognizing them. When you notice one, pause and reframe your thoughts in a more balanced way.

How might you overcome these setbacks? The first step in dealing with setbacks is awareness. Pay close attention to your thoughts, emotions, and the situations triggering your over-thinking. Keep a journal or use a mindfulness app to track your patterns. Understanding your triggers is half the battle.

Whenever you catch yourself in negative self-talk, add "yet" to your statements. For example, if you think, "I can't do this," change it to "I can't do this yet." This small word shift opens the door to growth and change, reminding you that progress takes time.

Challenge cognitive distortions with evidence-based thinking. When you find yourself catastrophizing, ask yourself, "Is this the worst thing that can happen, or am I exaggerating?" Seek out facts to ground your thoughts in reality.

Replace negative self-talk with positive, constructive messages. Instead of saying, "I'll never get this right," try, "I can learn from my mistakes and improve." Over time, these affirmations can reshape your mindset.

When you catch yourself overthinking, employ the 3-2-1 rule. Ask yourself three specific questions about the issue, consider two potential solutions, and then take one actionable step toward a resolution. This structured approach helps break the cycle of endless rumination.

Don't hesitate to reach out to a trusted friend, family member, or therapist when setbacks feel overwhelming. Sharing your thoughts and feelings with someone you trust can provide valuable insights and emotional support.

It's completely normal to face obstacles and setbacks along the way, but with these strategies and a bit of patience, you can make real progress. You've got the power to break free from the chains of overthinking, and every setback is just a stepping stone toward a more peaceful mind.

You're stronger than you think, and every small victory brings you closer to a brighter, more balanced mindset. Embrace these strategies, stay persistent, and watch as your overthinking gradually loosens its grip on your life. You've got this!

THE ACTION STEPS

The action steps will help you stop overthinking and find a more peaceful state of mind.

Self-reflection is key to making positive changes. Take a moment to think about your journey so far. What strategies have worked for you in the past? Which habits have been most effective in calming your mind? Write them down in a journal or a note on your phone. This simple act of self-reflection can be incredibly powerful.

But, let's be honest, we all have those areas where we still struggle. It's okay! No one's perfect, and it's all part of the process. Think about those areas where overthinking tends to creep in. Is it when you're making decisions, or maybe it's in your interactions with others? Identifying these triggers is a crucial step in overcoming them.

Just as equally important—your support system. Having people who believe in you and your mental health goals can make all the difference. Who are these people in your life? It could be a close friend, a family member, or even a colleague. Identify those individuals who genuinely care about your well-being and are willing to lend an ear when you need it.

Sometimes we hesitate to reach out to these supportive people, even though they want to help. Why is that? Fear of burdening them? Or maybe we're just not used to opening up? These are valid concerns, and I get it. Sometimes, we overthink about whether we should even bother them.

Studies have shown that having a support system can reduce stress and anxiety significantly (Reid, 2023). So, it's not just you who benefits from this connection, but your loved ones as well. It's a two-way street of love and support.

Ask yourself, "How can I connect with my support system more regularly?" Maybe it's a weekly catch-up call, a coffee date, or just a text to check in. Find what works for you, and don't hesitate to reach out. Remember, they want to be there for you.

As we wrap up this book, let's take a moment to reflect on your progress and review how to maintain the positive changes you've worked so hard to achieve.

Be mindful that you may slip back into old habits occasionally. You're only human, and overthinking is a pesky companion that can rear its head when you least expect it. The key is not to beat yourself up over these moments but to view them as opportunities for growth. Embrace the setbacks as part of your learning process.

This journey is not about perfection; it's about progress. Life will present you with countless opportunities to practice what you've learned. Overthinking may still knock on your door, but now you have the tools to politely escort it away.

I've shared my experiences and the insights I've gathered from scientific research, but the real hero of this story is you—the determined individual who decided to take control of their own thoughts and emotions.

CONCLUSION

As we draw the curtains on *Help Me Stop Overthinking*, let's take a moment to reflect on the transformative journey we've embarked on together. Over the course of this book, we've explored the labyrinth of overthinking, examining its roots, consequences, and most importantly, strategies to break free from its tenacious grip.

Overthinking is an insidious habit that many of us fall prey to. At its core, it's the act of ruminating on thoughts to an excessive degree. While a little introspection is healthy, when it veers into the territory of over-analysis, it can be paralyzing. We've understood that the roots of overthinking often lie in our insecurities, past traumas, or the fear of the uncertain future. This incessant rumination not only robs us of the joy in the present moment but also impairs our ability to make clear decisions, thus affecting various facets of our lives.

One profound realization we've encountered is the undeniable impact of overthinking on our mental health. Prolonged over-thinking can lead to heightened anxiety, stress, and even depression. It's a constant drain on our emotional energy, leaving us feeling exhausted and overwhelmed. The state of our mind has a ripple effect on our overall well-being, affecting our relationships, work, and even physical health.

But there's hope. This book has equipped you with a toolkit of strategies to tackle overthinking head-on. Whether it's grounding exercises, mindfulness techniques, or cognitive restructuring, these tools are designed to help you regain control over your thoughts. It's essential to revisit the final chapter regularly and ensure that you're actively using these techniques. Remember, knowledge without action is futile.

You must remember to be patient and kind to yourself. The healing from overthinking will not be an easy one, but it is an attainable one. Remind yourself that for each stumble, there is opportunity for growth. If you ever feel that you're sinking deeper into the abyss of overthinking despite your best efforts, do not hesitate to seek professional help. There's no shame in leaning on therapy or counseling. Sometimes, having an objec-tive listener can provide the clarity we often seek.

Thank you for accompanying me on this journey of self-discovery and growth. By sticking through to the end, you've shown immense determination and commitment to bettering yourself. I commend you for that. If you've found value in this book, I'd be honored if you took a moment to leave a review. Sharing your experiences and insights will not only help others on a similar journey but also serve as a reinforcement of your own learning.

Before we part, I'd like to introduce you to my other works, which might resonate with you:

- *Help Me Talk to Anyone*: A guide to improving your communication skills, breaking barriers, and expressing yourself with confidence.
- *Help Me, I'm Stuck:* Your roadmap to navigating life's challenges, finding purpose, and reigniting passion.

If you ever feel stuck in life or wish to hone your communication prowess, these resources could be your guiding light.

In conclusion, always remember that while thoughts are powerful, *YOU* have the power to control them. Equip yourself, stay grounded, and remember that every moment lived without overthinking is a moment lived to its fullest.

Until next time, stay present and cherish the now!

P.S. I left a little gift at the end of this book. Please enjoy.

GLOSSARY

All definitions were sourced from (Kaiser et al., 2015).

Amygdala: An almond-shaped cluster of nuclei in the brain involved in processing emotions, particularly fear and anxiety.

Analysis Paralysis: The state of overthinking a decision to the point of inaction or being unable to make a choice due to excessive analysis.

Cognitive Distortion: Distorted or irrational thought patterns commonly associated with anxiety and overthinking.

Cortisol: A stress hormone released by the adrenal glands in response to stress, which can have negative effects on the brain when chronically elevated.

Decision Fatigue: The deteriorating quality of decisions made by an individual after a long session of decision making, often leading to overthinking.

Dopamine: A neurotransmitter associated with reward and motivation; dysregulation can contribute to anxiety disorders.

Dorsolateral Prefrontal Cortex (DLPFC): A part of the brain associated with executive functions, including decision-making and impulse control, which can be affected by overthinking.

Executive Function: Cognitive processes responsible for planning, organizing, initiating, and completing tasks, often impaired in individuals who struggle with overthinking.

Fight-or-Flight Response: A physiological reaction that occurs in response to a perceived threat, involving the release of stress hormones.

Gray Matter: Brain tissue primarily composed of cell bodies of neurons, affected by chronic stress and anxiety.

Homeostasis: The body and brain's natural state of balance and stability, which can be disrupted by prolonged stress and overthinking.

Hippocampus: A region of the brain crucial for memory formation and retrieval, often affected by chronic stress.

Hypervigilance: A heightened state of alertness and sensitivity to potential threats, often associated with anxiety.

Hypothalamus: A brain region that regulates many bodily functions, including the stress response.

Information Overload: The state of being overwhelmed by excessive information, which can contribute to overthinking and decision-making difficulties.

Meta-Cognition: The process of thinking about one's own thinking, often leading to overanalyzing and overthinking various aspects of one's life.

Neurogenesis: The process of generating new neurons, which can be impacted by chronic stress.

Neurotransmitters: Chemical messengers in the brain, such as serotonin and dopamine, which play a role in regulating mood and stress.

Parasympathetic Nervous System: The branch of the autonomic nervous system responsible for calming the body's stress response.

Prefrontal Cortex: The part of the brain responsible for executive functions such as decision-making, problem-solving, and impulse control, often affected by overthinking.

Perseveration: The repetition of thoughts or behaviors, often seen in individuals who struggle with overthinking and are unable to let go of certain ideas.

Psychosomatic: Relating to physical symptoms or conditions influenced by psychological factors, often associated with chronic stress.

Rational Emotive Behavior Therapy (REBT): A therapeutic approach that helps individuals identify and challenge irrational beliefs and thought patterns, often used to address overthinking.

Reticular Activating System (RAS): A network of neurons in the brainstem that plays a role in regulating wakefulness and attention, impacted by stress and anxiety.

Rumination: The act of repetitively thinking about the same thoughts or problems, often associated with overthinking.

Selective Attention: The cognitive process of focusing on specific information while ignoring other distractions, which can be disrupted by overthinking.

Self-Criticism: The tendency to judge yourself harshly and engage in negative self-talk, which can exacerbate overthinking.

Serotonin: A neurotransmitter involved in mood regulation; imbalances are linked to anxiety and depression.

Synaptic Plasticity: The ability of synapses (connections between neurons) to change in strength, which can be influenced by stress and anxiety.

Thought Stopping: A cognitive-behavioral technique used to interrupt and replace repetitive, negative, or overthinking thoughts with more positive and constructive ones.

Uncertainty Tolerance: The ability to cope with and accept ambiguity and uncertainty, which is often reduced in individuals who engage in over-thinking.

Venting: The act of expressing one's thoughts and feelings as a way to release pent-up emotions and reduce overthinking.

White Matter: Brain tissue consisting mainly of axons (nerve fibers) that connect different regions of the brain; disruption can occur due to stress.

Worry: A form of thinking characterized by repetitive and often anxious thoughts about potential future problems or negative outcomes, closely related to overthinking.

Worst-Case Scenario Thinking: A cognitive bias where individuals focus on the most negative and unlikely outcomes, often contributing to excessive worry and overthinking.

Zeigarnik Effect: The psychological phenomenon where people tend to remember uncompleted or interrupted tasks better than completed ones, which can lead to overthinking about unfinished business.

REFERENCES

Ackerman, C. (2017, April 12). *28 benefits of gratitude & most significant research findings.* PositivePsychology.com. https://positivepsychology.com/benefits-gratitude-research-questions/

Acosta, K. (2022, January 11). *What causes overthinking—and 6 ways to stop.* Forbes Health. https://www.forbes.com/health/mind/what-causes-overthinking-and-6-ways-to-stop/

Amistad, L. (2023, February 15). *Screen time effects on mental health.* La Amistad. https://lamistad.com/blog/screen-time-effects-on-mental-health/

Anderson Witmer, S. (2023, March 24). *What is overthinking, and how do I stop overthinking everything?* GoodRx. https://www.goodrx.com/health-topic/mental-health/how-can-i-stop-overthinking-everything

Bartel, R. (2019, May 31). *Loving through boundaries.* ImpactBank. http://impactbank.ca/loving-through-boundaries/#:

Callesen, P. (2021, May 26). *How to stop overthinking.* Psyche. https://psyche.co/guides/how-to-stop-overthinking-with-help-from-metacognitive-strategies

Craft, L. L., & Perna, F. M. (2004). The benefits of exercise for the clinically depressed. *Primary Care Companion to the Journal of Clinical Psychiatry, 6*(3), 104–111. https://www.ncbi.nlm.nih.gov/pmc/articles/PMC474733/

Crego, A., Yela, J. R., Riesco-Matías, P., Gómez-Martínez, M.-Á., & Vicente-Arruebarrena, A. (2022). The benefits of self-compassion in mental health professionals: A systematic review of empirical research. *Psychology Research and Behavior Management, 15*(1), 2599–2620. https://doi.org/10.2147/PRBM.S359382

Escalante, A. (2021, January 28). *New science: Why our brains spend 50% of the time mind-wandering.* Forbes. https://www.forbes.com/sites/alisonescalante/2021/01/28/new-science-why-our-brains-spend-50-of-the-time-mind-wandering/?sh=6cd4192d4854

Editors of Psychology Today. (2021, September 23). *Default mode network.* Psychology Today. https://www.psychologytoday.com/intl/basics/default-mode-network

Harveston, K. (2022). *5 science-backed ways to stop overthinking.* Happify. https://www.happify.com/hd/5-science-backed-ways-to-stop-overthinking/

Hengen, K. M., & Alpers, G. W. (2021, February 22). *Stress makes the difference: Social stress and social anxiety in decision-making under uncertainty.* Frontiers. https://www.frontiersin.org/articles/10.3389/fpsyg.2021.578293/full#:

H. E. U., Quotes, 2022 C. I., & Development, P. (2019, April 17). *34 quotes to help you to stop overthinking (+ my 5 favorite tips).* The Positivity Blog. https://www.positivityblog.com/overthinking-quotes/

Hofmann, S. G., Asnaani, A., Vonk, I. J. J., Sawyer, A. T., & Fang, A. (2012). The efficacy of cognitive behavioral therapy: A review of meta-analyses. *Cognitive Therapy and Research, 36*(5), 427–440. https://doi.org/10.1007/s10608-012-9476-1

Jay, M. (2020, September 15). *What to do when your mind (always) dwells on the worst-case scenario.* Harvard Business Review. https://hbr.org/2020/09/what-to-do-when-your-mind-always-dwells-on-the-worst-case-scenario

Kaiser, B. N., Haroz, E. E., Kohrt, B. A., Bolton, P. A., Bass, J. K., & Hinton, D. E. (2015). "Thinking too much": A systematic review of a common idiom of distress. *Social Science & Medicine, 147,* 170–183. https://doi.org/10.1016/j.socscimed.2015.10.044

Kapil, R. (2022, March 14). *How and why to practice self-care.* Mental Health First Aid. https://www.mentalhealthfirstaid.org/2022/03/how-and-why-to-practice-self-care/#:

Kristenson, S. (2022, June 22). *104 mindfulness affirmations to live in the present moment.* Happier Human. https://www.happierhuman.com/mindfulness-affirmations/

Mayo Clinic. (2022, February 3). *Positive thinking: Stop negative self-talk to reduce stress.* Mayo Clinic. https://www.mayoclinic.org/healthy-lifestyle/stress-management/in-depth/positive-thinking/art-20043950

McEwen, B. S. (2017). Neurobiological and systemic effects of chronic stress. *Chronic Stress, 1*(1). https://doi.org/10.1177/2470547017692328

McLachlan, S. (2021, December 22). *The science of habit: How to rewire your brain.* Healthline. https://www.healthline.com/health/the-science-of-habit#1

Millson, A. (2022, August 11). *Thinking too hard really can make you tired, scientists say.* Bloomberg. https://www.bloomberg.com/news/articles/2022-08-11/thinking-too-hard-really-can-make-you-tired-scientists-say

Mitchell, S. (2023, March 28). *6 online communities for personal growth and healthy development.* MUO. https://www.makeuseof.com/online-communities-personal-growth-healthy-development/#:

Naidoo, U. (2016, April 13). *Nutritional strategies to ease anxiety.* Harvard Health. https://www.health.harvard.edu/blog/nutritional-strategies-to-ease-anxiety-201604139441#:

Neff, K. (2012, July 2). *The physiology of self-compassion.* Self-Compassion. https://self-compassion.org/the-physiology-of-self-compassion/

News In Health. (2019, February 28). *Practicing gratitude.* https://newsinhealth.nih.gov/2019/03/practicing-gratitude#:

Potts, Y. (2019, November 13). *The science of overthinking.* Woroni. https://www.woroni.com.au/words/the-science-of-overthinking/

Reid, S. (2023, March 2). *Social support for stress relief.* HelpGuide.org. https://www.helpguide.org/articles/stress/social-support-for-stress-relief.htm#:

Saripalli, V. (2022, February 22). *15 benefits of journaling and tips for getting started.* Healthline. https://www.healthline.com/health/benefits-of-journaling

Schechter, N. (2020, July 9). *15 signs you have relationship anxiety.* Netdoctor. https://www.netdoctor.co.uk/healthy-living/a33267326/relationship-anxiety/

Scroggs, L. (2022). *The pomodoro technique – why it works & how to do it.* Todoist. https://todoist.com/productivity-methods/pomodoro-technique

Stangor, C. & Walinga, J. (2014, October 17). *1.2 The evolution of psychology: History, approaches, and questions.* In *Introduction to psychology* (1st Canadian edition). BC Campus. https://opentextbc.ca/introductiontopsychology/chapter/1-2-the-evolution-of-psychology-history-approaches-and-questions/

Suni, E. (2016, November 14). *How does lack of sleep affect cognitive impairment?* Sleep Foundation. https://www.sleepfoundation.org/sleep-deprivation/lack-of-sleep-and-cognitive-impairment#:

WebMD Editors. (2021, October 25). *Mental health benefits of journaling.* WebMD. https://www.webmd.com/mental-health/mental-health-benefits-of-journaling#:

Wikipedia. (2022, December 2). *Cognitive bias.* Wikipedia. https://en.wikipedia.org/wiki/Cognitive_bias#:

IMAGE REFERENCES

Camargo, J. (2018). *Fountain pen, note, journal* [Image]. Pixabay. https://pixabay.com/vectors/fountain-pen-note-pen-journal-3409472/

Hassan, M. (n.d.). *Exhausted, stressed man walking* [Image]. Pixabay. Retrieved March 31, 2022, from https://pixabay.com/vectors/tired-exhausted-stress-man-walking-7103575/

Hassan, M. (2017). *Customer experience* [Image]. Pixabay. https://pixabay.com/illustrations/customer-experience-best-excellent-3024488/

Hassan, M. (2021a). *Ladder of success* [Image]. Pixabay. https://pixabay.com/vectors/ladder-of-success-success-goals-6585235/

Hassan, M. (2021b). *Mental therapy* [Image]. Pixabay. https://pixabay.com/vectors/mental-therapy-counseling-people-6841357/

Hassan, M. (2021c). *Self-love* [Image]. Pixabay. https://pixabay.com/vectors/self-love-myself-esteem-positive-6871019/

Hassan, M. (2022a). *Brain key* [Image]. Pixabay. https://pixabay.com/vectors/brain-key-mental-awareness-health-6927977/

Hassan, M. (2022b). *Headache, stressed, mental health* [Image]. Pixabay. https://pixabay.com/vectors/headache-stressed-mental-health-7220178/

Hassan, M. (2022c). *Keto diet* [Image]. Pixabay. https://pixabay.com/vectors/keto-diet-fat-low-cholesterol-7617639/

Hassan, M. (2022d). *Mirror, business man, self reflection* [Image]. Pixabay. https://pixabay.com/vectors/mirror-businessman-self-assurance-7677012/

Hassan, M. (2022e). *Overthink, question, doubtful* [Image]. Pixabay. https://pixabay.com/vectors/overthink-question-doubtful-7185863/

Hassan, M. (2022f). *Weight loss, run, treadmill* [Image]. Pixabay. https://pixabay.com/vectors/weight-loss-run-treadmill-woman-7323872/

Hassan, M. (2023a). *Counseling, therapy, mental health* [Image]. Pixabay. https://pixabay.com/vectors/counseling-therapy-mental-health-7717987/

Hassan, M. (2023b). *Development, watering head* [Image]. Pixabay. https://pixabay.com/vectors/brain-development-watering-head-7842215/

jambulboy. (2017). *Questions, man, head, answers* [Image]. Pixabay. https://pixabay.com/vectors/questions-man-head-success-lamp-2519654/

S7akti. (2022). *Women self-care* [Image]. Pixabay. https://pixabay.com/vectors/woman-self-care-care-self-love-6956139/

ALSO BY VAUGHN CARTER

Ever wanted to improve the quality of your relationships?
Look no further than *Help Me Talk to Anyone* to discover simple
ways to stop making the most common mistakes in
communication and learn how to easily connect with others.
Read on to sample the introduction…

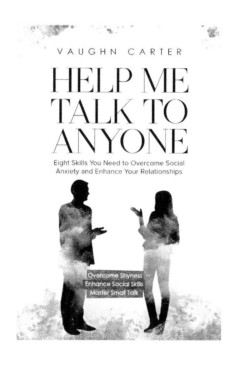

INTRODUCTION

Many years ago, I was invited to a cocktail party to meet new people and make some friends. Sounds fun, right? More like, *terrifying*. Back then, I would describe myself as a very shy and introverted person. I honestly would have enjoyed staying home and reading a good book. The complete series of Sherlock Holmes wasn't going to read itself, after all.

I also believed I couldn't communicate well with others on their level because of how nervous and anxious I was around new people and crowds. I remember the many thoughts running through my head:

- *What in the world are we going to talk about?*
- *What if it gets awkward?*
- *What if I put my foot in my mouth, again?*

Having lived with these nagging thoughts for most of my life, I made peace with the fact that I simply didn't have the needed conversation skills. It's hopeless. There's nothing I can do about it. That's *some* attitude I had!

Maybe you're wondering how a person like that would get invited in the first place.

Well, someone invited my older brother, and he wanted to help me break out of my shell. We were noticeably different when it came to talking to new people. He was blessed with *extroversion*, which, to me, felt like a superpower that I thought I would never attain myself.

People socially sought after him, and for good reason. He knew how to break the ice, connect easily with others, and could even entertain a whole crowd! So, naturally, I felt more confident around him. And if he was going, the cocktail party couldn't be all that bad, right?

The next thing I knew, we both got dressed up, and hit the road. For my brother, we were heading toward a good time. But for me, a disaster.

About two hours after we arrived, there I was: In the middle of the room, by myself, looking very awkward with a cocktail in hand and no one to talk to. My brother on the other hand, was busy making friends and living his best life.

What was his secret? I mean, *really*?

What was the difference between us two? More importantly, was that a skill I could master myself?

Was being an effective (and enjoyable) communicator possible for someone like me who was shy and reserved? Was I doomed forever?

Are you shy? Does the thought of talking to others make you anxious?

After that evening, I made it my mission to find ways to become a better conversationalist. It was a long and arduous road to improvement, and worth every bit of effort.

How often have you found yourself in a similar position where you feel it best to avoid these types of social scenarios?

The truth is most of us have a wealth of knowledge and a whole truckload of passion for interesting topics. Perhaps you just struggle to package it in a way that draws others in.

Have your friends or family pointed this out to you? Maybe, like me, they called you the shy one. Or they said on your behalf, "They are just quiet." It's not that you don't have something to say, but it's hard when you struggle to get your thoughts across. You have so much information stored up, but the neural connections in your brain don't want to help you relate it to others. And this might cause some anxiety, which stops you dead in your tracks. Like I said, I've been there.

Imagine yourself being a big part of the conversation. There you are, standing tall and looking confident in a small group of people you respect. You're telling your knockout story and building up to the best part. Everyone's eagerly anticipating what you will say next. As they hang on to every word, you dramatically pause before saying the most important part. As the story goes on, it's eating them up inside! The suspense is causing them to sweat. One lady passes out from all the excitement. A man in the group catches her just before she hits the ground. When she finally comes to, all she asks is, "How did the story end?"

With a smile, you kindly explain, "Well, I wouldn't want to bore you all by telling it again."

"No, please!" they say. "We would love to hear it again! Sarah, don't faint this time."

Poor Sarah.

End scene.

Was that a little over the top? Perhaps. A little dramatic? Maybe. But learning to speak to others is not just about exchanging words. We want to be *engaging* while we do it, to connect.

Imagine feeling excited instead of anxious whenever someone mentions a social or corporate gathering.

Imagine being the person in the room that everyone wants to talk to!

Wow. Feels amazing, right? That's exactly what this book will help you to do.

Thankfully, I've learned how to be an effective conversationalist shortly after I started putting value on myself and what I bring to the table. People have been paying more attention to me because I make sure I have something important and valuable to share. And now you can too!

I've gone through all of the same struggles of communicating that you might be experiencing. Maybe you've read other books to help you with this, but it didn't quite suit you. But this book? I share some of the fundamental secrets I've learned that are important for you to become a great conversationalist. Say goodbye to the shyness and lack of social skills and say hello to new friends and improved relationships. Learn how to master small talk and keep a conversation going. And so much more!

My name is Vaughn, and I'm a teacher, consultant, and the author of the best-selling book, *Help Me, I'm Stuck*, which focuses on improving your mindset.

My passion and drive to help others succeed motivated me to write this book. It's difficult to see others struggle with shyness and social anxiety after going through it myself. It's my earnest desire to support them.

In just eight chapters, I will help you improve your social skills, overcome social anxiety, and become the most sought-after person in the room. Just one question:

Are you ready?

Most popular titles

Printed in Great Britain
by Amazon

39335514R00088